System, Society and the World

Exploring the English School of International Relations

Second Edition

EDITED BY
ROBERT W. MURRAY

**E-INTERNATIONAL
RELATIONS
PUBLISHING**

E-International Relations
www.E-IR.info
Bristol, England
First published 2015

ISBN 978-1-910814-05-5 (paperback)
ISBN 978-1-910814-08-6 (e-book)

Copy Editing: Gill Gairdner
Production: Michael Tang
Cover image: TonyTaylorstock

A catalogue record for this book is available from the British Library.

E-IR Edited Collections

Series Editors: Stephen McGlinchey, Marianna Karakoulaki and Robert L. Oprisko

E-IR's Edited Collections are open access scholarly books presented in a format that preferences brevity and accessibility while retaining academic conventions. Each book is available in print and e-book, and is published under a Creative Commons CC BY-NC 4.0 license. As E-International Relations is committed to open access in the fullest sense, free electronic versions of all of our books, including this one, are available on the E-International Relations website.

Find out more at: http://www.e-ir.info/publications

Recent titles

Restoring Indigenous Self-Determination (new version)

Nations under God: The Geopolitics of Faith in the Twenty-first Century

Popular Culture and World Politics: Theories, Methods, Pedagogies

Ukraine and Russia: People, Politics, Propaganda and Perspectives

Caliphates and Islamic Global Politics (new version)

About the E-International Relations website

E-International Relations (www.E-IR.info) is the world's leading open access website for students and scholars of international politics. E-IR's daily publications feature expert articles, blogs, reviews and interviews – as well as a range of high quality student contributions. The website was established in November 2007 and now reaches over 200,000 unique visitors a month. E-IR is run by a registered non-profit organisation based in Bristol, England and staffed with an all-volunteer team of students and scholars.

Acknowledgements

I want to extend my sincerest thanks to E-International Relations for commissioning a second edition of this project. The faith that the entire E-International Relations team, especially Stephen McGlinchey, placed in this volume is unparalleled. I would also like to thank profusely the world-class collection of contributors to this volume, whose promptness and brilliance made the project worthwhile and who will hopefully provide students and scholars of the English School with food for thought. I am eternally grateful for the work and support provided to this project by Brianna Heinrichs, whose continual support is humbling.

Robert W. Murray is Vice-President of Research at the Frontier Centre for Public Policy and an Adjunct Professor of Political Science at the University of Alberta. He holds a Senior Research Fellowship at the Atlantic Institute for Market Studies and Research Fellowships at the University of Calgary's Centre for Military and Strategic Studies and University of Alberta's European Union Centre for Excellence. He is the co-editor of *Libya, the Responsibility to Protect, and the Future of Humanitarian Intervention* with Aidan Hehir (Palgrave, 2013), *Into the Eleventh Hour: R2P, Syria and Humanitarianism in Crisis with Alasdair MacKay* (E-International Relations, 2014), and *International Relations and the Arctic: Understanding Policy and Governance* with Anita Dey Nuttall (Cambria, 2014).

Abstract

Since its reorganisation in the early 1990s, the English School of international relations has emerged as a popular theoretical lens through which to examine global events. Those who use the international society approach promote it as a middle way of theorising due to its ability to incorporate features from both systemic and domestic perspectives into one coherent lens. Succinctly, the English School, or society of states approach of IR, is a threefold method to understanding how the world operates. In its original articulations, the English School was designed to incorporate the two major theories that were trying to explain international outcomes – namely, realism and liberalism. This second edition brings together some of the most important voices on the English School, including new chapters and insights from key English School scholars, to highlight the multifaceted nature of the School's applications in international relations.

Contents

This project is dedicated to all of those students and observers of international relations, past, present and future, seeking a middle way through the thicket of self-proclaimed truths.

Introduction

ROBERT W. MURRAY
FRONTIER CENTRE FOR PUBLIC POLICY AND UNIVERSITY OF
ALBERTA, CANADA

Most theories that examine the global arena focus on either one, or a small number of, issues or units of analysis to make their case about the nature or character of the global realm. While some theorists may desire alterations or a decline in the power of the state, states have not declined so far as to be removed from their place as the central actors in international relations. Even those efforts that aim at changing politics above the state level to focus more on humanity than purely state concerns often rely on states to implement new doctrines. The changes to interstate relations and the new issues facing the world at present require new ways of approaching international relations, without abandoning rational preferences completely. One often overlooked theoretical lens which could allow for the type of theorising required to encompass a more accurate evaluation of contemporary international relations is referred to as the English School.[1]

Succinctly, the English School, or society of states approach, is a threefold method for understanding how the world operates. In its original articulations, the English School was designed to incorporate the two major theories that were trying to explain international outcomes – namely, realism and liberalism. In order to come to a better, more complete understanding of IR, English School theorists sought to answer an essential question: 'How is one to incorporate the co-operative aspect of international relations into the realist conception of the conflictual nature of the international system.'[2] According to English School logic, there are three distinct spheres at play in international politics, and these three elements always operate simultaneously. They are, first, the international system; second, international society; and third, world society. Barry Buzan provides an explanation of each sphere:

1. International System (Hobbes/Machiavelli) is about power politics amongst states, and Realism puts the structure and process of international anarchy at the centre of IR theory. This position is broadly parallel to mainstream realism and structural realism and is thus well developed and clearly understood.

2. International Society (Grotius) is about the institutionalisation of shared interest and identity amongst states, and Rationalism puts the creation and maintenance of shared norms, rules and institutions at the centre of IR theory. This position has some parallels to regime theory, but is much deeper, having constitutive rather than merely instrumental implications. International society has been the main focus of English School thinking, and the concept is quite well developed and relatively clear.

3. World Society (Kant) takes individuals, non-state organisations and ultimately the global population as a whole as the focus of global societal identities and arrangements, and Revolutionism puts transcendence of the state system at the centre of IR theory. Revolutionism is mostly about forms of universalist cosmopolitanism. It could include communism but, as Wæver notes, these days it is usually taken to mean liberalism. This position has some parallels to transnationalism but carries a much more foundational link to normative political theory. It is the least well developed of the English School concepts and has not yet been clearly or systematically articulated.[3]

The English School incorporates realist postulates, such as an emphasis on the primacy of states interacting in an anarchic system, but combines that realist understanding with the notion of a human element emerging from the domestic sphere. Kai Alderson and Andrew Hurrell claim that 'international relations cannot be understood simply in terms of anarchy or a Hobbesian state of war'.[4] The most important element of the English School, international society, therefore operates based on the influence of both the international system (realism) and world society (revolutionism).

Within the English School itself there are two distinct divisions, which interpret the conduct and goals of international society very differently. The first is the *pluralist* account, which adheres to a more traditional conception of IR by placing its emphasis on a more Hobbesian or realist understanding of the field. Pluralists, according to Andrew Linklater and Hidemi Suganami, stress the conduct of states within anarchy but are still sure to note that states cooperate, despite the existence of self-interest.

> A pluralist framework places constraints on violence, but it does not outlaw the use of force and is, in any case, powerless to eradicate it … . War is not only an instrument of realist foreign policy but is also a crucial mechanism for resisting challenges to the balance of power and violent assaults on international society.[5]

The pluralist version of international society is founded upon minimalist rules, the protection of national sovereignty, and the quest to create and maintain international order. The constraints imposed on international society by the system of states and the condition of anarchy are thought to be the most important factors in explaining and understanding the conduct of a pluralist society of states, and such a close relationship to realist theory is what keeps the pluralist conception of the English School within a traditional IR framework.

The second interpretation of international society is referred to as the *solidarist* account. Solidarist conceptions of international society are interpreted in various ways, and can incorporate a variety of IR theories. Solidarists typically place their emphasis on the relationship between world society, or third level, and international society. In its earliest articulations, solidarism focused predominantly on Kantian or liberal understandings of IR, since the primary focus was on how the individual within the state affected the conduct of the society of states.[6] This allowed for notions such as human rights, individual security and peace to permeate the normative foundations of the international society.

Over time and since the end of the Cold War, the solidarist account of international society has also been used and interpreted by critical theorists, who want to maintain the state in their theory but find a way to include critical, global or human concerns. Barry Buzan argues:

> This view stresses global patterns of interaction and communication, and, in sympathy with much of the literature on globalization, uses the term society mainly to distance itself from state-centric models of IR … [world society] is aimed at capturing the total interplay amongst states, non-state actors and individuals, while carrying the sense that all the actors in the system are conscious of their interconnectedness and share some important values.[7]

The focus on individuals, norms, values and even discourse have come to provide a forum for liberal and critical projects in IR to use the English School as a method of both explaining and understanding the world from a perspective which does stray from realism but does not reject the primacy or necessity of the state in global affairs.

There is little doubt that the English School has grown in its popularity since the end of the Cold War, and the post-1990s period in English School theory has been termed as the School's 'reorganisation' by Buzan and other prominent scholars who adopt the international society approach. One of the most interesting elements of the School is the diversity of theoretical allegiances and geographical location of those who consider themselves to be within the School and the plethora of work done under the society of states banner over the last two decades.[8] A large advantage to a middle-approach like the English School is that on one level, it does incorporate the realist elements of IR with an emphasis on the state. On another level, however, the world society element of English School theory is able to allow for a wide array of theorists to discuss various critical elements and their effects on the society of states. Whether these come in the form of emancipation theory, globalisation theory, neo- or postcolonial theory or even postmodern thinking, the critical thinkers who choose to adopt an English School method are forced to ground their work in some understanding of the state or international society. Making sure that any contemporary efforts to examine the international arena can maintain traditional elements is an essential component of modern IR. Robert Jackson highlights this point as he states:

> Contemporary international relations theory tends to be a mixed bag of unrelated approaches which usually are not in dialogue. I would borrow less from unrelated disciplines and make better use of the abundant traditional resources which are available for theorizing contemporary problems of international relations seeking thereby to add to our accumulated historical stock of knowledge.[9]

As a result of such a pluralistic model, the English School can be said to represent a coherent and advantageous method for achieving a broad and complex understanding of modern international political issues.

To demonstrate the advantages and value of the English School, this second edition brings together some of the most important voices in the School to highlight the multifaceted nature of the School's applications in international relations. In a departure from typical academic literature, this compendium was assembled with the specific goal of introducing readers to the School's key elements in a way that would be accessible in terms of both comprehension and availability.

The second edition begins with a chapter by Filippo Costa Buranelli that traces the current state of the English School. Costa Buranelli discusses at length the various incarnations and applications of the English School in the broader context of international theory and how the different sub-schools within the English School are growing. According to Costa Buranelli, there are three distinct ways in which the modern English School is being used by various scholars – the first being discussions of norms and institutions; the second pertaining to methods; and the third being historical. Costa Buranelli argues that the English School is thriving now more than ever.

In attempting to explain how the English School is best positioned to explain events and trends in an evolving state system, Cornelia Navari emphasises the School's engagement with world society. Navari's discussion of the School's methodological focus on participant observation make the world society level of theorising more apt in explaining the causes of change, rather than strictly the sources of change, as humanity's impact of world events continues to grow.

In his reassessment of a pivotal piece of international relations literature, Richard Little traces the impact of Bull and Watson's *The Expansion of International Society* on international relations and the English School. Little examines the criticism of Eurocentrism levelled against Bull and Watson's vision of international society and is sure to highlight the duality of European dominance and the trend of imitation employed by non-European powers in their entrenchment into the society of states.

In the first of the new contributions for the volume's second edition, Ian Hall traces the history of the English School and focuses on how early School thinkers interpreted diplomacy. Hall conveys the message that early English School thinkers understood diplomacy in such a way, namely intersubjectivity, that has had a profound impact on the evolution of English School thought. According to Hall, core School concepts such as normativity, morality and statespersonship have all been influenced by the School's early interpretivism, though more modern School thinkers have divided into two distinct groups that have each moved away from this early thought process. Hall's chapter concludes by encouraging those reading the School to think of it more in terms of different approaches rather than assuming, as some suggest, that the entire School embraces methodological pluralism.

Andrew Linklater's chapter presents a discussion of civilisations in the history of international society. Linklater comments on the importance of civilisations in Wight's initial conceptions of how and why international societies work, and perhaps most importantly, interrogates the need for a re-evaluation of civilisational study as new centres of power outside of the West look likely to influence international society in the future.

Building on the impact of shifts in international power, Roger Epp focuses his attention on the role of China in international relations theory. Epp's primary contention is that the English School is well suited to take up discussions about China's influence on IR theory, and how the School's interpretive and historical elements would be ideal for analysing emerging trends in Chinese IR theory.

Adrian Gallagher's contribution explores one of the pivotal characteristics of English School study: human rights. Gallagher claims that the School's work on human rights has been an essential influence on international relations, primarily because of its ability to balance optimism and pessimism. As Gallagher suggests, the middle way promoted by the School has allowed it to critically examine rights and responsibilities issues in the broader context of IR, and has done so very well.

Cathinka Vik uses the English School framework to demonstrate that no simple answers exist when attempting to explain the American response to genocide in Rwanda. Vik's ultimate contention is that of all theoretical approaches to the questions surrounding American inaction in Rwanda, the propensity for tension in the international order can be well addressed by the English School given its multi-layered theoretical orientation.

Building on themes introduced by Gallagher and Vik, Tim Dunne provides a useful narrative on the English School's relationship with enforcing human rights via humanitarian intervention. With poignancy, Dunne notes the differentiations between pluralist and solidarist conceptualisations of humanitarian actions, as well as the institutional and normative challenges facing states acting in instances of egregious human rights abuses. Dunne describes the evolution of interventionism that has more recently focused on the Responsibility to Protect (R2P) and how the English School is well equipped to explain how and when R2P is both useful and necessary, given the constraints and challenges it faces. For Dunne, a key component of taking R2P more seriously and putting it into action stems from what he calls a 'pluralist defence of responsibility'.

In an effort to demonstrate the regional aspects of English School theory, Yannis Stivachtis provides a study of some of the most important regional or sub-global international societies in the world today. As the world continues to move away from a Europe-centric conception of international society, Stivachtis contends that regional international societies will become increasingly apparent and important. The extension of international society theory to the regional level is one of the innovative ways the School has contributed to empirical studies in recent years, and Stivachtis has been at the forefront of this work.

As the international system evolves, the rise of new great powers has become an increasingly important theme of international relations study. Jason Ralph's chapter investigates the role of the BRICS states and how useful the English School can be in exploring their impact on international affairs. By attempting to balance the themes of 'prestige in numbers' with an interpretation of legitimacy contingent upon efficacy, Ralph argues that BRICS members may be able to further increase their roles in international decision-making, and if too much prominence continues to be granted to the efficacy-based model of legitimacy without consideration of numbers, the School's conservative image may endure.

In his chapter, Matthew Weinert delves into a crucial aspect of the English School's framework, world society. Weinert astutely questions what precisely is meant by a world society and who the members of world society may be. His conclusion is a novel contribution to the School, contending as it does that theorists must question how to 'make human', and the five mechanisms proposed help scholars do just that: reflection on the moral worth of others, recognition of the other as an autonomous being, resistance against forms of oppression, replication (of prevailing mores), and responsibility for self and others.

In his examination of the English School's pluralist and solidarist accounts of international society, Tom Keating presents the value of a balanced and pluralistic approach to constructing the identity of a given society of states. Keating notes that the most powerful explanation for why states continue to pursue coexistence in international society is due to the ongoing stability provided by pluralist concerns in state sovereignty without a total abandonment for solidarist values such as rights.

In another of the chapters produced for the second edition of the volume, John Williams builds on many of the ideas proposed in Keating's chapter but takes a very different view of pluralism within the School. Williams takes exception to the traditionally empiricist and state-centric conceptualisation of English School pluralism, noting quite rightly that pluralists define international society too narrowly and overlook important international variables such as non-state politics, political economics, and cosmopolitan ethics. From this contention, Williams presents a notion of pluralism grounded on a more robust normative agenda predicated on the idea of ethical diversity. Such a theoretical reorientation, argues Williams, would assist pluralism in providing a more useful contribution to English School theory.

Alexander Astrov builds on a point introduced by Keating, noting the role and influence that great powers play in the society of states. Of all the institutions studied by English School scholars, Astrov argues, great power management is in need of elaboration. Astrov's analysis of what exactly is meant by 'management' in a system of independent states all with the power of consent, leads to a fundamental and important interrogation of exactly what role great powers play in the function of international society.

In a meta-theoretical investigation of the methodological limitations of the English School, Robert Murray presents the argument that, due to the proliferation of scholars employing the School, the time may have come for a more defined set of boundaries to establish exactly what distinguishes an English School theory. To do so, Murray proposes the use of Imre Lakatos' work on Scientific Research Programmes to assist in the identification of the School's hard-core assumptions and test contributions to the School for whether they are, in fact, adding value.

In all, these outstanding pieces clearly demonstrate the value and vibrancy of the English School as it exists today. Spanning a wide array of issues and themes, this second edition intends to provoke thought about the School's value and possible ways forward and provide new insights into contemporary challenges and issues of international relations in both theory and practice. There is no doubt these objectives are achieved and will hopefully contribute to the development of the English School of international relations theory and compel students and observers of international politics to see greater explanatory and theoretical value in the idea of international society.

Notes

1. For a comprehensive introduction to, and historical account of, the English School, see Tim Dunne, *Inventing International Society: A History of the English School* (Houndmills: Palgrave, 1998).
2. B.A. Roberson, 'Probing the Idea and Prospects for International Society', *International Society and the Development of International Relations Theory* (London: Continuum, 2002), 2.
3. Barry Buzan, 'The English School: an underexploited resource in IR', *Review of International Studies* 27:3 (2001), 474.
4. Kai Alderson and Andrew Hurrell, 'Bull's Conception of International Society', *Hedley Bull on International Society* (Houndmills: Macmillan, 2000), 4.
5. Andrew Linklater and Hidemi Suganami, *The English School of International Relations: A Contemporary Reassessment* (Cambridge: Cambridge University Press, 2006), 131.
6. Ole Wæver, 'International Society: Theoretical Promises Unfulfilled?', *Cooperation and Conflict* 27:1 (1992), 98.
7. Barry Buzan, *From International to World Society? English School Theory and the Social Structure of Globalization* (Cambridge: Cambridge University Press 2004), 64.
8. For a comprehensive bibliography of English School sources, see 'The English School of International Relations Theory', http://www.polis.leedsac.uk/research/

international-relations-security/english-school/ (accessed January 25, 2013).

9. Robert Jackson, 'Is there a classical international theory?', *International theory: positivism and beyond* (Cambridge: Cambridge University Press, 1996), 216.

1

The State of the Art of the English School

FILIPPO COSTA BURANELLI
KING'S COLLEGE LONDON, UK

2016 marks the 35th anniversary of one of the most famous antagonistic quotes in the discipline of International Relations (henceforth IR). In 1981, in the pages of the *Review of International Studies*, Roy Jones argued for the 'closure' of the English School, due to its lack of coherence as a research programme, the vagueness of its aims, the poorness of its methodology and the disputable status of the School as a 'theory'.[1]

Today, not only is the School still open but it has strengthened its position in academia and academies,[2] it is in dialogue both with other theories in IR and with other disciplines outside the domain of IR, it is becoming more and more fertile in terms of research programme and output, it is in tune with contemporary events and it is even rediscovering its original historical vein.

Proof of this may be found in the following elements: a compendium published for the International Studies Association (ISA),[3] a new introductory book published by Barry Buzan,[4] an increase in membership in the English School section of the ISA and the establishment of four fully operative working groups with world-wide membership: on the Institutions of International Society, on Regional International Societies, on Solidarism and Pluralism in International Society, and on the History of International Society.

Without neglecting significant criticism and legitimate disagreements on some of the tenets of the theory,[5] the turning point of the revitalisation of this school of thought (I have chosen this term to satisfy also those allergic to theory not concerned with strict causation) is a famous paper presented by Barry Buzan at the British International Studies Association (BISA).[6] Since then, the

English School has engaged with numerous debates within IR and been able to provide insightful contributions and additional research material to both young and established scholars. In this chapter, I will focus on the most recent ones.

The first new research agenda, inaugurated in 2009 by Buzan's and Gonzalez-Pelaez's book on the Middle East,[7] is undoubtedly the regional one. Departing from the global level of analysis, dear to the first generation of scholars, English School research has recently focussed on the regional level of analysis, applying socio-structural theory of norms and institutions at the sub-global level. Insightful and innovative pieces of work have been produced by a variety of scholars on a variety of regions: Europe,[8] Scandinavia,[9] Latin America,[10] East Asia,[11] Eurasia,[12] African Union members,[13] the Arctic[14] and Central Asia.[15]

The merits of this agenda are evident. First, it contributes to a more refined and more theoretically grounded understanding of how norms and institutions are framed, localised and understood in contexts that may be markedly different from the solidarist, liberal Western 'global level'; in this respect, a much welcomed special issue of *Global Discourse* edited by Yannis Stivachtis critically considers the very existence of a 'global' international society.[16] Second, it brings the English School outside the domains of Eurocentrism. This is something to cherish, especially given the Eurocentric character of its historical production.[17] Third, it adds to the wider academic field of comparative regionalism, emphasising neither institutional design[18] nor forms of cooperation[19] but primary institutions and socio-structural dynamics.

The second agenda inaugurated, coincidentally again in 2009, is the one on methods. As we have mentioned above, methods have been the Achilles heel of the School for a long time. However, the project convened by Navari et al. has systematised the methodological (dispersed) pluralism of the School into a coherent toolkit, with better specified epistemological and methodological assumptions and more refined methods of analysis.[20] This agenda is by no means exhausted, with works currently being produced on causation and even possible dialogue with process-tracing.[21]

The third agenda, which brings the English School 'back to the roots', is the historical one. English School scholars have (re)started exploring different international societies across history,[22] adding original research to the narrative of the 'expansion of international society',[23] focussing on world society and its impact on the normative structure of international society in given historical times.[24] This is a very welcome development of English School research as it positions the School as a valid platform (but by no means the only one) to facilitate dialogue between International Relations and History.

The fourth and last agenda, to demonstrate the vitality and fertility of the School, is concerned with the relationship between *primary* institutions (meant as durable, routinised practices such as sovereignty, diplomacy and international law) and *secondary* institutions (meant as international organisations, such as the UN or ASEAN). Following the work of Buzan[25] and Holsti[26] on how these two ontologies are related, Knudsen[27] and Spandler[28] have provided new theoretical insights insisting on the mutual relationship between these two categories: if primary institutions give birth and make possible secondary ones, it is also true that secondary ones may shape and modify primary ones. In this respect, Cornelia Navari has convened a research project studying international organisations through the theoretical prism of primary institutions called 'International Organisations in the Anarchical Society'.

All this is promising and certainly discourages new calls for closures. Nonetheless, it is important to discuss what the importance of the English School is. Why should a first-year student be interested in it? The answer lies in three of its features: holism, poly-methodology and a historical vein paired with normative reasoning and problematisation. I will dig deeper into each of these features.

By holism I simply mean the denial that either agency or structure have precedence in determining the course, the content and the characteristics of world politics. International politics, and especially international society, defined as an arrangement with which states regulate their relations through the use and the common understanding of norms, rules, practices and institutions, is the result of the co-constitution of the agents giving birth to the structure and the structure constituting the roles, the behaviours and the identities of agents. With its emphasis on institutions, the English School allows students and scholars alike to avoid the narrowness of reductionist theories and the deterministic fetishism of structural theories (mostly neorealism and neoliberalism).

The co-constitution of international society and its members, therefore, allows scholars to approach world politics both from the bottom up (how states and individuals sustain, challenge and modify the content and the practice of international society) as well as from the top down (how states and individual conform to and are constituted by the social web of norms, rules and practices informing international relations). This, as is evident, is a characteristic that the English School shares with constructivism, and parallels between the two have been already noticed elsewhere.[29] It goes without saying that this approach to world politics, relying on both structure and agency and on their co-constitution, is better equipped to explain 'change' in world politics: of identities, of practices, of values.

Moving to the issue of methodology, the English School's renovated interest for methods has already been noted above; nevertheless, it is important to specify that given the plurality of methods available to English School scholars, any research programme conducted using English School theory will inevitably benefit from a polyphony of sources and data, not necessarily available (or, even worse, interesting) to other theories. As a postulate, it follows that such variety of methods encourages, by definition, a dialogue with other disciplines outside the IR ivory tower but nonetheless tangential, such as history, sociology, international political economy, security studies,[30] linguistics[31] and anthropology.[32] There is also an aspect related to cultural sensitivity, particularly in Asia, where the School is diffusing: despite criticism to its Eurocentric epistemology and overall an expression of Western (theoretical) domination, the English School is considered also open to non-Westphalian politics and is, therefore, anti-hegemonic.[33]

The third aspect of the English School that makes it appealing to young students and established scholars working in this tradition is its sensitivity to history, the relationship between history, the present and normative reasoning. Unlike realism, which studies history to find and prove recurrent patterns of states' behaviour in world politics, and differently from liberalism,[34] which tends to study history in a progressive and teleological way, the English School studies history in its own right, focussing on orders, patterns of relations, practices and institutions as arising, deceasing and evolving over time.

This historical sensitivity is always accompanied by a desire, a need, an impulse to trace the normative foundations of (historical) international societies. Attention to the values, the priorities, the moral philosophy underpinning relations between states has always been a feature of any English School research programme (and, again, one of its peculiarities as compared to realism and liberalism in their neo- variants and constructivism, which are much more interested in epistemological questions than in normative ones).

In fact, the recent research on regions and non-Western international organisations outlined above has shown how values, political priorities and conceptualisations of legitimacy vary across cultures, regions and social systems. Yet, discussions on human rights,[35] humanitarian intervention,[36] the benefits of a pluralist order[37] and the ethical consequences of borders and territoriality[38] signal that:

> The English School is grounded in the practical, in the real-world tussle of power and interests, while at the same time it works through what is possible to say about the nature of obligation and moral responsibility among international actors. This is where ethics and practical interest meet, and it represents the unique contribution of the English School to contemporary normative IR theory.[39]

Indeed, an English School approach to the study of the Global Financial Crisis, the massive influx of refugees in Europe and the expansion of the Islamic State/ISIS illuminates important questions concerning the legitimacy, the viability and the practicality of the practices sustaining contemporary international society, with a specific emphasis on the institutions of sovereignty, borders, the market, humanitarian intervention and the protection of the state system itself.

The road ahead

From what was discussed above, it is clear that the English School has resisted well to criticism and calls for closure over the years, refining some of its under-specified aspects without losing its central identity. Not only is it an ecumenical school of thought able to dialogue with several disciplines and other schools of thoughts in international relations, but it has also been able to bring about a coherent and multifaceted research programme thanks to its ontological and methodological pluralism, as well as thanks to the fruitful synergy between senior and junior scholars.

Yet, as Jorgensen has astutely observed, 'the English School is currently in an interregnum between orthodoxy and innovation',[40] and therefore challenges still lie ahead. For example, the School has yet to provide for what really counts as a primary institution of international society. This is, in fact, a largely under-researched aspect of English School theory, albeit work on this has recently commenced.[41] Also, the study of interregional societies remains largely unexplored, despite tentative initial research.[42]

The next years will test the School's ability to live up to its new, promising research agendas. Yet, the sizzling community that is forming across the globe, paired to innovative and fresh theorisation well in tune with a solid tradition of thought, is certainly reason for hope, as this book reflects.

Notes

1. Roy E. Jones, 'The English school of international relations: a case for closure', *Review of International Studies*, 7, 1 (1981), pp. 1-13.

2. Tim Dunne asserts that three indicators demonstrate that the English School has been taken increasingly seriously in the global IR epistemic community since the publication of his 'Inventing International Society': influential textbooks on IR theory now include a chapter on the ES (pedagogical indicator); leading IR journals, notably RIS and Millennium, and the influential CUP/BISA series have consistently published increasing number of works on the ES (editorial indicator); and the fact that 'beyond its heartland, there is significant interest in its [ES] work in continental Europe as well as the USA, Canada, Australia, China and India (epistemic/academic indicator). Tim Dunne, *Inventing International Society: A History of the English School* (St. Martin's Press, 1998); Tim Dunne, 'The English School' in *The Oxford Handbook of International Relations* ed. Christian Reus-Smit and Duncan Snidal (Oxford: Oxford University Press, 2008); Tim Dunne, 'The English School' in *International Relations: Discipline and Diversity* ed. Tim Dunne, Milja Kurki and Steve Smith (Oxford: Oxford University Press, 2010).

3. Cornelia Navari and Daniel Green, *Guide to the English School of International Studies* (London: Wiley Blackwell, 2014).

4. Barry Buzan, *An Introduction to the English School of International Relations: The Societal Approach* (London: John Wiley & Sons, 2014).

5. Martha Finnemore, 'Exporting the English School?', *Review of International Studies*, 27, 3 (2001), pp. 509-13; Daniel Copeland, 'A realist critique of the English School', *Review of International Studies*, 29, 3 (2003), pp. 427-41.

6. Barry Buzan, 'The English School as a Research Program: An Overview, and a Proposal for Reconvening', paper delivered to the panel 'A Reconsideration of the English School: Close or Reconvene', BISA (Manchester, 1999).

7. Barry Buzan and Ana Gonzalez-Pelaez, *International society and the Middle East: English School Theory at the Regional Level* (Basingstoke: Palgrave Macmillan, 2009).

8. Yannis A. Stivachtis, 'Civilization and international society: the case of European Union expansion', *Contemporary Politics*, 14, 1 (2008), pp. 71-89.

9. Laust Schouenborg, *The Scandinavian international Society: Primary Institutions and Binding Forces, 1815–2010* (London: Routledge, 2012).

10. Federico Merke, 'The Primary Institutions of the Latin American Regional Interstate Society', LSE IDEAS Papers, London 2011.

11. Barry Buzan and Yongjin Zhang, *Contesting International Society in East Asia* (Cambridge: Cambridge University Press, 2014).

12. Georgeta Pourchot and Yannis A. Stivachtis, 'International society and regional integration in Central Asia', *Journal of Eurasian Studies*, 5, 1 (2014), pp. 68-76; Katarzyna Kaczmarska, 'Russia's droit de regard: pluralist norms and the sphere of influence', *Global Discourse*, 5, 3 (2015), pp. 434-48.

13. Elaine Tan Shek Yan, *Understanding African International Society: An English School Approach*, PhD thesis (Aberystwyth: Aberystwyth University, 2013).

14. Robert W. Murray, *Arctic International Society: Applying the English School to the High North*, International Studies Association (New Orleans, LA, 2015).

15. Filippo Costa-Buranelli, *International Society and Central Asia*, PhD thesis (London: King's College, 2015).

16. Yannis A. Stivachtis, 'Interrogating Regional International Societies, Questioning the Global International Society [Special Issue]', *Global Discourse*, 5, 3 (2015), pp. 327-517.

17. Hedley Bull and Adam Watson, *The Expansion of International Society* (Oxford: Clarendon Press, 1984).

18. Amitav Acharya and Alastair Iain Johnston, *Crafting Cooperation: Regional International Institutions in Comparative Perspective* (Cambridge: Cambridge University Press, 2007).

19. Philippe De Lombaerde and Michael Schulz, *The EU and World Regionalism: The Makability of Regions in the 21st Century* (London: Ashgate Publishing, 2009).

20. Cornelia Navari, *Theorising International Society* (Houndmills: Palgrave, 2009).

21. Charlotta Friedner Parrat, 'Changing before our eyes and slipping between our fingers: international organisations and primary institutions', International Studies Association, Annual Conference (Toronto, ON, 2014); Filippo Costa-Buranelli, 'Explaining the Yolks: Process-tracing and the Formation of Regional International Societies', paper presented at the workshop on regional international societies at Roskilde Universtity (Roskilde, 2015).

22. Alex Aissaoui, *System or Society? Ancient Near Eastern Polities (ca. 1600–1200 BCE)* International Studies Association (San Francisco, CA, 2013).

23. Carsten-Andreas Schulz, 'Civilisation, barbarism and the making of Latin America's place in 19th-century international society', *Millennium: Journal of International Studies*, 42, 3 (2014), pp. 837-59; Filippo Costa-Buranelli, 'Knockin' on Heaven's door: Russia, Central Asia and the mediated expansion of international society', *Millennium: Journal of International Studies*, 42, 3 (2014), pp. 817-36.

24. John Anthony Pella Jr, 'World society, international society and the colonization of Africa', *Cambridge Review of International Affairs*, 28, 2 (2015), pp. 210-28.

25. Barry Buzan, *From international to World Society?: English School Theory and the Social Structure of Globalisation* (Cambridge: Cambridge University Press, 2004).

26. Kalevi Jaakko Holsti, *Taming the Sovereigns* (New York: Cambridge University Press, 2004).

27. Tonny Brems Knudsen, *Fundamental Institutional Change at the UN and the ICC: Solidarist Practices of Law and War* International Studies Association (New Orleans, LA, 2015).

28. Kilian Spandler, 'The political international society: change in primary and secondary institutions', *Review of International Studies*, 41, 3 (2015), pp. 601-22.

29. Christian Reus-Smit, 'Constructivism and the English School', *Theorising International Society* ed. Cornelia Navari (Houndmills: Palgrave, 2009).

30. Barry Buzan, 'The English School: a neglected approach to international security studies', *Security Dialogue*, 46, 2 (2015), pp. 126-43.

31. Filippo Costa-Buranelli, '"Do you know what I mean? Not exactly!" English School, regional international societies and the polysemy of institutions', *Global Discourse*, 5, 3 (2015), pp. 499-514.

32. Nicolàs Terradas, *Anarchical Societies: Anthropological Investigations* BISA (London, UK, 2015).

33. Yongjin Zhang, 'The global diffusion of the English School' in *Guide to the English School in International Studies* ed. Cornelia Navari and Daniel Green (London: Wiley, Blackwell, 2014).

34. David C. Kang, 'An East Asian international society today? The cultural dimension'

in *Contesting International Society in East Asia* ed. Barry Buzan and Yongjin Zhang (Cambridge: Cambridge University Press, 2014).

35. R.J. Vincent, *Human Rights and International Relations* (Cambridge: Cambridge University Press, 1987).

36. Nicholas J. Wheeler, *Saving Strangers: Humanitarian Intervention in International Society* (New York: Oxford University Press, 2003).

37. Jason G. Ralph, *Defending the Society of States: Why America Opposes the International Criminal Court and its Vision of World Society* (New York: Oxford University Press, 2007).

38. John Williams, *The Ethics of Territorial Borders: Drawing Lines in the Shifting Sand* (Basingstoke: Palgrave Macmillan, 2006).

39. Molly Cochran, 'Normative theory in the English School' in *Guide to the English School in International Studies* ed. Cornelia Navari and Daniel Green (London: Wiley Blackwell, 2014).

40. Knud Erik Jørgensen, "Things are different in Pago Pago': a rejoinder to Ahrens and Diez', *Global Discourse*, 5, 3 (2015), pp. 356-9.

41. Peter Wilson, 'The English School meets the Chicago School: the case for a grounded theory of international institutions', *International Studies Review*, 14, 4 (2012), pp. 567-90.

42. Thomas Linsenmaier, 'The interplay between regional international societies', *Global Discourse*, 5, 3 (2015), pp. 452-66.

2

World Society and English School Methods

CORNELIA NAVARI
UNIVERSITY OF BUCKINGHAM, UK

The English School in IR theory is generally associated with the notion of international society. Indeed, it is often referred to as the international society approach. Its emblematic text is Hedley Bull's *Anarchical Society*[1], where Bull contrasted British approaches to international relations with those American and realist approaches where states are driven solely by power politics and egoistic materialism, the only laws being 'the laws of the jungle'. Bull argued that although the international realm could be typified as anarchical in the sense of lacking an overarching authority to define and enforce rules, it did not mean that international politics were anarchic or chaotic. Contrary to the billiard-ball metaphor of international politics, states are not just individual elements in a system. In practice, there is a substantial institutionalisation of shared values, mutual understandings and common interests; hence, the 'anarchical society'. Indeed, he argued that even ethics were an integral part of world politics, and that prudence and morality were not mutually exclusive.

'International society' is currently understood in two senses. On the one hand there are its fundamental or 'primary' institutions, as Barry Buzan has distinguished them.[2] These are its bedrock institutions, which Buzan has characterised as agreed practices that have evolved over time. Originally identified by Hedley Bull, there were five sets of practices that contributed to maintain order in international society: diplomacy, international law, great power management, power balancing and the regulated use of force (or simply 'war' as Bull understood the term). Buzan has recently added the market, reflecting the developing institutions underpinning globalisation and K. J. Holsti has added colonialism, a tendency in which he includes humanitarianism and rights interventionism.[3] These practices exist as habits and common understandings, with a few rules. But they are also institutionalised in 'secondary' institutions – international organisations such as the United Nations. The best known example is the requirement for Security Council concurrence to initiate measures to protect the peace and punish offenders of civilian immunity in wartime, which is an institutional -isation of great power management.

As developed by Hedley Bull, an international society was to be contrasted with an international 'system'. In a system, patterns of regular behaviour could be observed, such as during the Cold War when the United States and Soviet Union avoided interfering in one another's blocs or spheres of influence. But such evidence of mutual restraint should not be taken to be signs of an emerging society since they were not underpinned by joint values or mutual understandings. They were the result of fear, or a prudent calculus on interests, likely to change as interests changed. As Barrie Paskins has observed, a 'community of terror' is not a community.[4] By contrast, the understandings underpinning an international society represent deep values, such as the value of sovereignty or the value of international law, unlikely to change (or at best to undergo slow evolution.)   Equally, however, an international society does not imply a deep commitment to communal values. If one contrast was with a system, the other was with a 'community'. In an 'international community', mutual understandings have developed to the point of shared goals and common world visions. A society, as understood by Bull, is characterised only by a shared view of proper procedures, and by procedural norms, not by shared ends. Barry Buzan has made a contrast between a 'thin' international society, such as represented in the United Nations, with a 'thick' international society as represented by the European Union.[5] Some would argue that the European Union is well on the way to becoming a true international community, with a common vision of the political good and a common defence system, common laws and agreed adjudication, leaving behind the idea of self-help that marks an international society.

Buzan has also been at the forefront in developing the idea of a world society, the term he prefers to that of 'international community'. A true world society is marked by 'the global identities of individuals'. It has less to do with how states behave than how individuals perceive their identities — whether, for example, young persons in Britain conceive of themselves as European as well as, or instead of, British. Buzan calls it 'the idea of shared norms and values at the individual level but transcending the state.'[6] It is constituted by the global societal identities and arrangements of individuals, non-state organisations and the global population as a whole; and it would be institutionalised in a wealth of non-governmental organisations, such as Oxfam or Doctors without Borders or the International Society of Authors.

Navari has explored the explanatory preferences of the classical English School theorists as they appear in the classic texts.[7] She agrees that the ideas of system, society and community can be used as structural concepts, each related to different modes of action; she also agrees that they are at the centre of the English School approach. But she observes that the classical theorists did not initially employ their structural concepts in a causal mode. They did not originally look for the causes of events, such as the causes of wars, at least not as 'causality' is understood in the formal literature. Their explanations, she points out, are generally in the *intentional mode*; that is, they explain events and outcomes by reference to the main actors' aims and intentions. She observes that the classical English School thinkers distinguished between mechanistic (causal) outcomes and chosen (intentional) outcomes: for Herbert Butterfield, Martin Wight and other 'founding fathers', an international *society*, as opposed to a system, was primarily the product of choices, and not causes.[8] Accordingly, she has identified the classical approach as 'participant observation'. In this approach, the research explains the conduct of foreign policy by observing the formulators of that policy and by gaining an understanding of their intentions.

There are, however, other distinct approaches in the English School armoury, which relate to different research concerns. Hidemi Suganami, who first suggested the title 'British Institutionalists' for the School,[9] has pointed to its concern with institutions. The fundamental or primary institutions of international society such as diplomacy, international law, the balance of power and state sovereignty are regularised and partly institutionalised practices. These would be identified by their regulatory rules, such as the rules for receiving diplomats or the rules on the extra-territoriality of an embassy. A second set is those of Robert Jackson, who has identified the English School's subject more broadly as 'codes of conduct'.[10] His focus is not so much with institutions as with the practices of 'statespersons' to discern their normative content. The questions he asks are, for example, how does a UN agent dealing with refugees understand his or her responsibilities, and to whom or what do they consider themselves responsible? A third focus is that of Richard Little and Barry Buzan who are concerned not with actors but with 'environments of action'. They argue that the central concepts of English School thought – international system, international society, and world society – are different environments of action, different social realities ('structures' in the contemporary parlance), which exist in a dynamic relationship with one another and which require incorporation into the consideration of conduct.[11] In short, Suganami emphasises institutions; Jackson emphasises agents; and Little and Buzan emphasise structures.

If the focus is institutions and rules, then one approach would be via international law. Peter Wilson has explained the English School understanding of international law, distinguishing between Positive Law – law that has emerged – and Aspirational Law – laws and procedures that may be emerging.[12] To determine whether a substantive institution has emerged, the researcher should ask whether institutional developments, such as human rights, contain definite obligations, whether they are sufficiently defined to allow a judge to determine derogation, and whether derogation gives rise to a sanction of some sort. To determine whether a substantive new institution is taking shape, the researcher should ask whether resolutions lead to further elaborations in later resolutions, and whether the endorsement of a new institution is hearty or sincere, on the part of a government or population of a state (Navari has recently used the model to evaluate the emerging democracy norm[13]). This is classic institutional analysis as understood in political science.

If the focus is on codes of conduct, then the procedure would be, as Robert Jackson has explained, the personal interview where the research interrogates the subject's reason for acting. In this method, the interviewer takes an 'insider view'; and he relates the present concerns of the subject to the classic concerns of statesmanship, such as how to understand security, or how to construct a balance of power to achieve stability.[14]

Richard Little has justified the use of varied approaches by reference to the underlying understandings of the classical English School theorists. According to Little, the classical English School theorists identified the reality of international relations with a 'diversity of action arenas', not merely with 'international society', and these insights are embedded in traditional English School habits of analysis — notably, different methods as applicable to different levels of analysis and to different forms of social structure. In consequence, he maintains that methodological pluralism is a necessary entailment, and a necessary requisite, of the English School approach, depending on the emphasis of the individual analyst and his or her particular research question.[15]

Little's schema draws directly on the notions of international system, international society and world society, respectively. He argues that each of these settings has different methods appropriate to its analysis: cost-benefit analysis in the context of a system of states; institutional analysis and comparative analysis in the context of a society of states; and institutional analysis and normative argument in the context of world society.

Buzan has gone further and proposed that Little's structure may be used to identify not only the sources of change in international society but also the identification of the causes of change. Elaborating on the concept of 'world society', he has argued that international society is not a way station on the historical road from anarchy to a world society but rather that an international society cannot develop further without parallel development in its corresponding world society; that is, by the development of elements of 'world culture' at the mass level. But he has also argued, in the manner of Hedley Bull, that a world society cannot emerge unless it is supported by a stable political framework and that the state system remains the only candidate for this.[16] The methodological implications are that 'world society' should be the focus of study, both as an object of growth and development and also as a source of change, but within the context of a (changing) state system.

Notes

1. Hedley Bull, *The Anarchical Society: A Study of Order in World Politics* (London: Macmillan, 1977).
2. Barry Buzan, *From International to World Society: English School Theory and the Social Structure of Globalization* (Cambridge: Cambridge University Press, 2004), 161-204.
3. K.J. Holsti, *Taming the Sovereigns: Institutional Change in International Politics* (Cambridge: Cambridge University Press, 2004).
4. Barrie Paskins, 'A Community of Terror?', in *The Community of States*, ed. James Mayall (London: Allen & Unwin, 1982), 85-95.
5. Barry Buzan, 'The English School: an underexploited resource', *Review of International Studies* 27:3 (2001), 487.
6. Buzan, 'English School: an underexploited resource', 477; see also John Williams, 'The International Society–World Society Distinction', in *Guide to the English School in International Studies,* eds Cornelia Navari and Daniel M. Green (Oxford: Wiley, 2014), 127-42.
7. Cornelia Navari, 'What the Classical English School Was Trying to Explain and Why its Members Were not Interested in Causal Explanation', in *Theorising International Society: English School Methods*, ed. Cornelia Navari (Basingstoke: Macmillan, 2008), 39–57.
8. See *Diplomatic Investigations*, eds Herbert Butterfield and Martin Wight (London: George Allen & Unwin, 1966) for the early writings of the 'founding fathers'.
9. Hidemi Suganami, 'British institutionalists, or the English School, 20 years on', *International Affairs* 17:3 (2003), 253-72.
10. Robert Jackson, *The Global Covenant: Human Conduct in a World of States* (Oxford: Oxford University Press, 2000).
11. Richard Little, 'International System, International Society and World Society: A Re-evaluation of the English School', in *International Society and the Development of International Theory*, ed. B.A. Roberson (London: Pinter, 1998), 59–79; Richard Little, 'History, Theory and Methodological Pluralism in the English School', in *Theorizing International Society: English School Methods*, ed. Cornelia Navari (Basingstoke: Macmillan, 2008), 78-103; Buzan, *From International to World Society*.
12. Peter Wilson, 'The English School's Approach to International Law', in *Theorizing*

International Society: English School Methods, ed. Cornelia Navari (Basingstoke: Macmillan, 2008), 167–88.

13. Cornelia Navari, 'Liberalism, Democracy and International Law: An English School Approach', in *After Liberalism*, eds Rebekka Freedman, Kevork Oskanian and Ramon Pacheco (Oxford: Oxford University Press, 2013).

14. Robert Jackson, 'The Classical Approach as a craft discipline', in *The Global Covenant* (Oxford: Oxford University Press, 2000), 77-96.

15. Little, 'History, Theory and Methodological Pluralism'.

16. Buzan, 'English School: an underexploited resource', 486.

3

Reassessing *The Expansion of International Society*

RICHARD LITTLE
UNIVERSITY OF BRISTOL, UK

The expansion of the international society as articulated by the English School is, arguably, the only effective and generally accepted grand narrative that prevails in international relations. Nevertheless, it has come under increasing criticism in recent years for its putatively pronounced Eurocentric bias.[1] There is, of course, a powerful school of thought that argues that such criticisms are inevitable because grand narratives are inherently suspect.[2] Indeed, according to Andrew Linklater, there is now 'a consensus' across the social sciences that regards any attempt to develop a grand or meta-narrative as profoundly regressive, although he also acknowledges that in recent years the importance of grand narratives has started to be reasserted.[3] It is timely, therefore, to reassess this particular grand narrative.

The narrative is very closely associated with the English School because Hedley Bull and Adam Watson, two of its key members, edited *The Expansion of International Society* – a seminal text that provides a detailed and extensive examination of how the modern international society emerged and evolved.[4] According to Brunello Vigezzi, the book is the English School's 'most organic and coherent achievement.'[5] But it is important to recognise that Bull himself identified the expansion narrative as the 'standard European view', not one distinctive to English School thinking.[6] Moreover, Bull and Watson were also quite open about its Eurocentric character, insisting that 'it is not our perspective, but the historical record itself that can be called Eurocentric'.[7]

Bull and Watson, however, fail to identify succinctly the constituent elements of this 'standard account', although it seems to follow the line that the contemporary international society originated in Europe where over several centuries a unique society of states evolved. Only in Europe did states exchange diplomatic missions in order to symbolise and ensure a continuity in relations, build up a body of international law to regulate relations among states and, more specifically, thereby dictate the terms under which war could be conducted – and, moreover, only in Europe did statesmen self-consciously begin to think in terms of a balance of power, with the great powers eventually managing their collective relations in order to preserve the balance.[8] Elements of these key institutions may be found elsewhere but this repertoire of institutions has to be regarded as unique to Europe.

The 'standard account' then assumes that this extensively developed international society became the prototype for the contemporary global international society and, on the face of it, what Bull and Watson wanted to do, therefore, was to map in more detail how this European society expanded outwards to become the basis for the contemporary global international society of sovereign states.

In fact, the picture that emerges from the large number of chapters that appear in Bull and Watson's text is much more complex than the standard account allows and, indeed, Bull insists that the standard account manifests obvious 'absurdities', such as the idea that ancient states like China, Egypt and Persia only became sovereign entities when they joined the European international society.[9] It is also relevant to note that initially the first generation of English School scholars were primarily interested in examining these earlier historical manifestations of international society formed in various places around the globe in order to establish a better understanding of the contemporary international society.[10] They came to focus on the expansion of international society project only because the task of providing a comparative historical study of international societies appeared to be too ambitious.[11]

Significantly, Bull and Watson also acknowledge that contemporary Third World or Developing World states challenge the 'standard account' of the expansion story because these states have refused to accept that they were only recently admitted into a European international society and speak instead of their 're-admission to a general international society of states and peoples whose independence had been wrongfully denied.'[12] In other words, Bull and Watson were fully aware of the argument that the European international society had at some point distanced itself from a broader international society that the European states had previously been members of. The implications of this argument are examined more fully below.

A close reading of Bull and Watson indicates that their grand narrative does, in practice, substantiate this view of Third World states. Certainly their analysis fails to endorse the 'standard account', at least in the form that I have outlined here. Instead, they insist that Europe did not evolve institutions and then export them. On the contrary, the expansion of Europe and the evolution of its international society are treated as 'simultaneous processes, which influenced and affected each other.'[13] Although they never systematically explore the full implications of this proposition, the text does illustrate this interactive process in the analysis of the later stages of European expansion.

To demonstrate this point, it is necessary to identify two distinct and important moves made in the text. The first move involves the recognition that the narrative must start long before most assessments of when the European international society came into existence. Rather than being a product of the sixteenth or seventeenth century it is necessary to trace developments over more than a thousand years. For most of this time Christendom and then Europe was only a minor player within Eurasia and as contact with other international societies across Eurasia increased so there was no alternative but to accommodate to the rules that governed these other international societies. The details of this long historical period are, however, only lightly sketched in Bull and Watson and most of the text focuses on a second move that makes the point that it was only in the nineteenth century that members of the European international society began to promote their own status and in doing so denigrate members of the other Eurasian international societies. From this perspective then, the contemporary global international society is very much a product of the nineteenth century.

It follows that the narrative that emerges in Bull and Watson is very much at odds with traditional thinking in international relations. The best-known date associated with the emergence of the modern international society is 1648 in the wake of the Treaty of Westphalia, although this assessment is now often considered to be a myth and there is growing support from a variety of sources for the idea that the modern international society only emerged in the nineteenth century.[14] But in any event, for Bull and Watson it is necessary to start the story very much earlier than the nineteenth century or even the seventeenth century and they begin by examining the territorial growth of Latin Christendom. With this first move there is also the acknowledgement that at that time there existed a range of discrete regional international societies that included the Arab-Islamic system, the Indian subcontinent, the Mongol Tartars on the Eurasian steppes, and China. Apart from the Eurasian steppes, all these regional international societies retained their independent identity into the nineteenth century, although by the end of that century they had all collapsed and the member states had been co-opted into an emerging global international society dominated by Europeans.[15]

Watson notes that Latin Christendom expanded initially into the peripheries of what came to be known as Europe, and then this colonisation process later embraced the Americas, so they too 'became an extension of Christendom.'[16] But what Watson fails to note is that at the same time the other international societies he identifies were following a very similar route of expansion.[17] It was only in the nineteenth century that it became apparent that Europeans had developed the potential capacity to influence in a very significant way all areas of the globe.

Long before the era of European overseas expansion, however, Christendom had already extended its borders very substantially. As Bartlett shows, Latin Christendom virtually doubled in size between 930 and 1350.[18] So the process of European empire building began within Europe and only later did the process extend overseas. But from an English School perspective it is also important to recognise that the process of European expansion evolved along a very distinctive track. The other Eurasian international societies are all identified as suzerain state systems, with the component states subordinate to a suzerain or hegemonic state. By contrast, throughout Europe's history as a distinct region there was always a plurality of competing states, and despite recurrent attempts by a number of these states to establish a hegemonic or suzerain status across Christendom, none was ever successful.

Yet, paradoxically, there is no substantial attempt in Bull and Watson to examine the idea of Europe as a distinctive system of empires. Of course, there has been some discussion of empires in the IR literature, particularly in recent years, but virtually no analysis of a society of empires, apart from a very brief discussion in Wight where he talks about secondary states systems made up of empires (or suzerain state systems, in his terminology).[19] But the only examples given disappeared long before the emergence of Christendom. Significantly, there is simply no acknowledgement by Wight, or within the field more generally, that the prevailing international society of states is the product of a society of empires and that this transformation is a very recent development. Nor was there any attempt by the first generation of English School scholars to explore the role that the colonies played in the development of the European international society. Within the English School this is now recognised as a major shortcoming.[20]

Yet from the start, the dominant units in Christendom and the nascent European international society were empires, engaged in a process of colonisation. Because there is no engagement with this development in Bull and Watson, there is no discussion of how the formation of empires played a crucial role in the transformation of the hierarchically structured Christendom through to the anarchically structured international society.[21]

This oversight, however, is not particularly surprising because it is no more than a reflection of the hegemonic dominance of the 'Westphalian myth' that prevailed at that time, not only in the study of international relations, but across the social sciences and humanities. As David Armitage notes,

> the rise of nationalist historiography in the nineteenth century had placed the history of the nation-state at the centre of European historical enquiry and distinguished the state from the territorial empires that preceded it, and in turn from the extra-European empires strung across the globe.[22]

The 'myth' presupposes that in 1648 a society of sovereign states emerged in Westphalia and this society eventually extended across the globe. As a consequence, the vital link between empires and states has simply not been observed in international relations. But as Armitage argues, more recently it has started to be acknowledged that empires 'gave birth to states and states stood at the heart of empires. Accordingly the most precocious nation-states of early-modern Europe were the great empire-states: the Spanish monarchy, Portugal, the Dutch Republic, France and England (later Britain).'[23] Yet, because nation-states and empires are conventionally treated as opposing political structures, the role of empires in the development of the European international society of states has been either ignored or left perennially ambiguous in most fields of study. Even so, the failure in Bull and Watson to interrogate the relationship between states and empires more closely remains odd, because Heeren's *History of the Political System of Europe and Its Colonies* written at the start of the nineteenth century places the colonies at the heart of the story and this was a book that both Bull and Watson greatly admired.[24] Indeed, Heeren's concept of a states system can be seen as the precursor and source of the English School's concept of an international society.

Prior to the nineteenth century, however, European colonisation remained very circumscribed. Despite the fact that from the sixteenth century onwards, the Europeans acquired increasing control over the oceans and seas around the globe they lacked the ability to penetrate the landmasses in Africa, Eurasia and the Americas (apart from Mexico and Peru). Instead they operated largely on the periphery of all these continents where they 'were accepted by the indigenous communities on a basis of equality as useful trading partners'.[25]

Bull and Watson's first move leads to the conclusion, therefore, that it is possible to identify the emergence of 'a loose Eurasian system or quasi-system' within which the European states 'sought to deal with Asian states on the basis of moral and legal equality.'[26] Bull and Watson do not describe this Eurasian system as a full-blown international society but it is certainly depicted as a nascent international society.

As a consequence, at the start of the nineteenth century the Europeans still acknowledged that they operated in a global arena where groups of states operated according to their own distinctive norms and institutions. Nevertheless, the Europeans were also to some extent integrated into these societies as either equals or subordinates. The ability of the Europeans to engage in trade and diplomacy around the world on the basis of signed agreements, therefore, provides evidence of a nascent global international society beginning to emerge.

Bull and Watson's second move relates to developments that took place during the course of the nineteenth century when they identify a dramatic transformation in the fundamental features of global international relations.[27] One aspect of this transformation relates to technological advances. According to O'Brien, these advances permitted, first, pronounced and widespread falls in freight rates, with '(q)uantum and qualitative leaps forward in international economic relations.'[28] Only at this point, according to O'Brien, is it possible to envisage the emergence of a worldwide economic system. Second, the development of steam power made it possible for the Europeans to penetrate the interior of Africa and China up their major rivers. Where there were no available rivers, the 'speed of rail construction was astonishing.'[29] Third, quick-firing, long-range firearms developed although Howard argues, fourthly, that improvements in 'European medical techniques' were even more crucial for European penetration of Africa and Asia.[30]

None of these developments by themselves had to lead to a transformation in international relations. They could simply have led to an intensification of established relations within the nascent global international society. But the impact of these developments was ratcheted up because they were accompanied by some equally remarkable changes in the self-image of the Europeans and Americans. It was this factor that proved crucial in transforming the nature of an evolving global international society.

According to Ian Brownlie, European and American international lawyers helped to precipitate and facilitate this change. By the middle of the nineteenth century it was agreed that state personality was determined by a collective recognition of statehood, but 'recognition was not dependent upon any objective legal criteria'.[31] Whereas it was assumed that the European and

American states – erstwhile members of Christendom – possessed state personality, large numbers of non-European political entities that had been treated as sovereign in the past were not now considered eligible to acquire statehood.

The justification for this development is linked to the increasing reference to 'modern civilised states' by nineteenth century international lawyers. But Brownlie is quite clear that the change, in practice, 'interacted with an increase in European cultural chauvinism and racial theories.'[32] Vincent argues that whereas there was a 'relative lack of colour consciousness among Europeans in earlier ages of expansion' in the nineteenth century, Europe was responsible for 'racializing the world'.[33]

The potential for a nascent global international society made up of large numbers of the existing political units around the world was essentially killed off. It was argued that to acquire statehood, and be permitted to enter the European international society, political entities had to measure up to a European standard of civilisation, despite the fact that, as Bull notes, the European states themselves could not live up to every aspect of this standard.[34]

This second move reveals that European expansion and the evolution of the international society were closely interlinked.[35] But Bull and Watson argue that it is important not to overplay this line of argument because it has the effect of removing any sense of agency from non-European actors. As Howard notes, the Russian response in an earlier era had been to 'imitate' the Europeans because they wished to be able to compete more effectively with the Europeans and they then constituted a vanguard that others could follow.[36] States like the Ottoman Empire, Japan and the Chinese Empire are shown to have followed the same route during the nineteenth century. Moreover, they also very quickly began to translate European and American international law textbooks and this helped them to assert their rights against the Europeans.[37] On the other hand, there were now also many independent political units that had been acknowledged as equals in an earlier era but were soon to be absorbed into the expanding European empires and successfully prevented, at least for the time being, from participating in the evolving European based international society.

Although it remains the case that the Europeans, but now more especially the Americans, are still endeavouring to employ their own cultural norms and institutions to define the essential features of the global international society, these endeavours have always been challenged and there is no doubt that the contemporary structure of the global international society is essentially multicultural in orientation. In Bull and Watson there are two chapters that explore this phenomenon and they come to diametrically opposed conclusions. Adda Bozeman argues that the brief historical period when Western norms and institutions prevailed has gone and this poses a fundamental challenge for European and American diplomacy, with Western diplomats having to function as they did before the nineteenth century 'in a world that has no common culture and no overarching political order, and that is no longer prepared to abide by western standards of international conduct'.[38] By contrast, Ronald Dore argues that there is a need to distinguish between universal and idiosyncratic values and interests and he is convinced that despite the obvious existence of diversity there are universal values that underpin an emerging world culture.[39]

Thirty years after *The Expansion of the International Society* was published, this debate remains as germane as ever. But it is also clear that the debate is more complex than is presented in Bull and Watson. Bozeman's assumes that the Western values that prevailed in the nineteenth century were essentially benign, whereas elsewhere in the book it is made clear that these values promoted the deeply problematic notion of a standard of civilisation that in practice reflected an essentially racist view of the world. By the same token, it is also far from clear that there is a set of universally accepted values in our contemporary world. Nevertheless, it remains the case that a careful reading of Bull and Watson indicates that they established a framework for thinking about international relations that was highly distinctive at the time it was written and retrospectively can be seen to have opened up avenues of thought that remain remarkably prescient and relevant.

Notes

1. See Turan Kayaoglu, 'Westphalian Eurocentrism in International Relations Theory', *International Studies Review* 12:2 (2010), 193-217; and Shogo Suzuki, Yongjin Zhang and Joel Quirk, eds, *Before the Rise of the West*.
2. See Jean-Francois Lyotard, *The Postmodern Condition: A Report on Knowledge,* trans. Geoff Nennington and Brian Massumi (Manchester: Manchester University Press, 1984).
3. See Andrew Linklater, 'Grand Narratives and International Relations', *Global Change, Peace and Security* 21:1 (2009), 3-17; and David Armitage, 'What's the Big Idea? Intellectual History and the *Longue Durée*', *History of European Ideas* 38:4 (2012), 493-507.
4. Hedley Bull and Adam Watson, eds, *The Expansion of International Society* (Oxford: Clarendon Press, 1984).
5. Brunello Vigezzi, *The British Committee on the Theory of International Politics (1954–1985): The Rediscovery of History,* trans. Ian Harvey (Milan: Edizioni Unicopli, 2005), 86.

6. Hedley Bull, 'The Emergence of a Universal International Society', in *Expansion of International Society*, eds Bull and Watson, 123.

7. Hedley Bull and Adam Watson, 'Introduction', in *Expansion of International Society*, eds Bull and Watson, 2.

8. The list reflects the five institutions – diplomacy, international law, war, balance of power and great power management – that constitute an international society in Hedley Bull, *The Anarchical Society* (London: Macmillan, 1977).

9. Bull, 'Universal International Society', 123.

10. See Brunello Vigezzi, *The British Committee on the Theory of International Politics, 1954–1985* (Milan: Edizione Unicopli Srl, 2005); and also Adam Watson, *The Evolution of the International Society: A Comparative Historical Analysis*, 2nd edition (London: Routledge, [1992] 2009).

11. Adam Watson did go on to develop a comparative historical study of international societies. See Watson, *The Evolution of the International Society.*

12. Bull and Watson, 'Introduction', 8.

13. Ibid., 6.

14. See, in particular, Barry Buzan and George Lawson, *The Global Transformation: History, Modernity and the Making of International Relations* (Cambridge: Cambridge University Press, 2015).

15. See David Gillard, 'British and Russian Relations with Asian Governments in the Nineteenth Century', in *Expansion of International Society*, eds Bull and Watson, 87.

16. Adam Watson, 'European International Society and Its Expansion', in *Expansion of International Society*, eds Bull and Watson.

17. See David A. Ringrose, *Expansion and Global Interaction 1200–1700* (New York: Longman, 2001).

18. Robert Bartlett, *The Making of Europe: Conquest, Colonization and Cultural Change 950–1350* (London: Penguin Books, 1994).

19. See Martin Wight, *Systems of States* (Leicester: Leicester University Press, 1977).

20. See Edward Keene, *Beyond the Anarchical Society: Grotius, Colonialism and Order in World Politics* (Cambridge: Cambridge University Press, 2002); and Barry Buzan, *From International to World Society: English School Theory and the Social Structure of Globalization* (Cambridge: Cambridge University Press, 2004).

21. Jeremy Larkins, *From Hierarchy to Anarchy: Territory and Politics Before Westphalia* (Basingstoke: Palgrave Macmillan, 2010).

22. David Armitage, *The Ideological Origins of the British Empire* (Cambridge: Cambridge University Press, 2000), 14.

23. Ibid., 15.

24. Richard Little, 'The Expansion of the International Society in Heeren's Account of the European States-system', Working Paper No. 07-08, School of Sociology, Politics and International Studies, University of Bristol, 2008.

25. Michael Howard, 'The Military Factor in European Expansion', in *Expansion of International Society*, eds Bull and Watson, 34.

26. Bull and Watson, 'Introduction', 5.

27. See Buzan and Lawson, *The Global Transformation,* who argue that the field of International Relations has failed to take account of the transformation of international relations in the nineteenth century but accept that in Bull and Watson there is an acknowledgement of this transformation.

28. Patrick O'Brien, 'Europe in the World Economy', in *Expansion of International*

Society, eds Bull and Watson, 50.

29. Howard, 'Military Factor in European Expansion', 39.

30. Ibid., 38.

31. Ian Brownlie, 'The Expansion of International Society: The Consequences for International Law', in *Expansion of International Society*, eds Bull and Watson, 362.

32. Ibid.

33. R.J. Vincent, 'Racial Equality', in *Expansion of International Society*, eds Bull and Watson, 241.

34. Bull, 'Universal International Society', 125.

35. This point has been greatly expanded in recent literature. See Anthony Anghie, *Imperialism, Sovereignty and the Making of International Law* (Cambridge: Cambridge University Press, 2004); Jordon Branch, " 'Colonial Reflection' and Territoriality: The Peripheral Origins of Sovereign Statehood", *European Journal of International Relations* 18:2 (2012) 277-297; and Lacy Pejcinovic, *War in International Society* (London: Routledge, 2013).

36. Howard, 'Military Factor in European Expansion', 36.

37. Gerrit W. Gong, 'China's Entry into International Society', in *Expansion of International Society*, eds Bull and Watson, 180-181; Hidemi Suganami, 'Japan's Entry into International Society', in *Expansion of International Society*, eds Bull and Watson, 195; Bull, 'Universal International Society', 121.

38. Adda Bozeman, 'The International Order in a Multicultural World', in *Expansion of International Society*, eds Bull and Watson, 406.

39. Ronald Dore, 'Unity and Diversity in Contemporary World Culture', in *Expansion of International Society*, eds Bull and Watson, 407-424.

4

Interpreting Diplomacy: The Approach of the Early English School[1]

IAN HALL

GRIFFITH UNIVERSITY, AUSTRALIA

In its first phase, which is normally dated from about 1959 to 1984,[2] the scholars who came to be labelled the early English School (ES), including Hedley Bull, Herbert Butterfield and Martin Wight, did not devote much effort to spelling out their preferred approach to international relations, let alone a research method. To make matters worse, the style and focus of their works varied, making it harder to distil an approach or method than it sometimes is when dealing with other schools of thought in International Relations (IR).[3] But there are similarities in the essays and books produced by the early ES, and there were common commitments, and this chapter tries to tease them out.

In general, the early ES took an 'interpretive' approach that concentrated on the beliefs of individual actors in international relations, assuming that explaining and evaluating their actions depends on interpreting the meaning they had for the actors who performed them.[4] This approach entailed, as Herbert Butterfield and Martin Wight wrote in the preface to *Diplomatic Investigations*, a focus on 'the diplomatic community', which they – in contrast to some later ES thinkers – took to be synonymous with 'international society' and 'the states-system'.[5] Butterfield, Wight, et al. were interested in 'the nature and distinguishing marks' of that community of individual actors, 'the way it functions, the obligations of its members, its tested and established principles of political intercourse', arguing that it carried with it 'an historical deposit of practical wisdom' called 'statecraft' that had 'lessons in relation to contemporary needs'.[6] And they were concerned 'to clarify the principles of prudence and moral obligation which have held together the international society of states throughout its history, and still hold it together.'[7]

This approach was followed in *Diplomatic Investigations*, but also in a number of other contemporary works, including the early essays of Wight's erstwhile student at the London School of Economics (LSE), Coral Bell, as well as her brilliant study of American strategic policy debates in the 1950s, *Negotiation from Strength* (1962); Peter Lyon's *Neutralism* (1963), which also began life at the LSE under Wight's supervision; Butterfield's *International Conflict in the Twentieth Century* (1960); and Wight's essays in the *Survey of International Affairs* for March 1939 (1952) or occasional pieces like 'The Power Struggle at the United Nations' (1956), and of course his late 1950s *International Theory* lectures, published posthumously in 1990.[8]

Underlying these works was an assumption that explaining and evaluating social behaviour depends on interpreting the meanings that behaviour has for actors and those with whom they interact. This entails a focus on social institutions, the bundles of norms and practices that have intersubjectively agreed meanings for actors in a given social group. In international relations, this involved a focus on the particular social institutions that have been emerged over time for the management of the interactions of states, or, to be more specific, for the management of the interactions of the rulers and representatives of states, as well as of their citizens. An interpretive approach also entails a focus on theories that espouse alternative norms and practices to those currently in operation, which some actors develop and utilise to contest the agreed norms and practices that make up social institutions. To explain and evaluate international relations, in other words, meant interpreting what key institutions meant to key actors, as their understandings and appraisal of the norms and practices of those institutions shaped their behaviour. And it meant interpreting the alternative norms and practices that at a given moment were being advanced by others, because they ideas can be taken up by actors and used to change key institutions, dispense with old ones, or create new ones.[9]

This approach is neatly displayed by Butterfield and Wight's contributions to *Diplomatic Investigations*, and to a lesser extent in Hedley Bull's 'The Grotian Conception of International Society', as well as Wight's *International Theory* lectures. Throughout, as Bull put it, their object was to find, 'the essence of ... [a] doctrine' espoused by an individual actor – whether a thinker or a practitioner – and to assess its impact on political practices of politicians and diplomats in international society.[10] Thus Butterfield, in 'The Balance of Power', scoured European intellectual history to locate the first iteration of the modern 'doctrine of balance', not merely to narrate the history of the idea but also to try to determine how it shaped the conduct of European statecraft.[11] In so doing, Butterfield inferred 'that an international order is not a thing bestowed by nature, but is a matter of refined thought, careful contrivance and elaborate artifice'.[12]

These processes – and the international orders that have been and could be generated by them – were also explored in detail in Wight's three essays, 'Why is there no International Theory?', 'Western Values in International Relations', and 'The Balance of Power'. His opening observation in the middle essay that the concept of 'Western Values' was itself a contrivance and artifice clearly signalled the intent not merely to describe a school of abstract thought, but to show how it shaped the practice of 'statesmen' seeking to maintain an international society, keep order, and uphold certain norms and moral standards.[13]

As Roger Epp has rightly argued, this approach to analysing international relations has 'strong resemblances' to Hans-Georg Gadamer's hermeneutics, which begins with the recognition that we are all located in traditions of thought that provide us with concepts with which to interpret the world around us, that past or different traditions need to be interpreted into our languages if we are to understand them, and that recognition that 'all understanding is interpretation'. Epp observes that the early ES also focuses on the languages of traditions because those scholars believes that they were 'constitutive rather [than] instrumental … bound up with practices and institutions … not simply the rationalisation or mystification of "interests"'.[14] Interpreting past and present languages of diplomacy was, for them, the core task of international relations theory, because those languages shaped the past and present conduct of their speakers and interlocutors. Or, as Epp puts it, this approach is necessary because, for the early ES, 'international society is a matter of intersubjective meaning embedded in practice'.[15]

This mode of explaining social behaviour – interpreting the beliefs of individual actors about the meanings of their actions – fell out of fashion in the later ES, as it did more broadly in the social sciences in the second half of the twentieth century.[16] It was utilised (albeit semi-consciously or unselfconsciously, and to a lesser or greater extent) in a series of works produced in the 1970s and 1980s by students or followers of the early School, but it was then set aside, for the most part, during the revival of the ES by a new generation of scholars in the mid-1990s.[17] This new generation maintained an interest in the history of ideas, but turned to other ways of explaining and evaluating the behaviour of actors in international relations more in keeping with their training as social scientists than those of the scholars in the early ES, who were mostly historians and philosophers.

In the new School, one wing has confined itself to evaluation and especially to normative theorising, drawing inspiration especially from post-Marxist critical theory. Andrew Linklater has been pivotal here, as he displaced Wight's earlier account of what he called 'revolutionism', associated with Immanuel Kant, but also with Karl Marx and even Adolf Hitler, with a positive 'revolutionist' vision of a cosmopolitan international society.[18] The aim of this wing of the School is to help realise this progressivist vision (or a version of it) by way of normative critique and prescription.

The other wing of the new School went in a quite different direction. It chose to explore the structure of international society, past and present, by utilising explanatory theories drawn from other social scientific traditions, notably functionalism, which is prominent in Bull's *The Anarchical Society* (1977), structural realism and neoliberalism, which play significant roles in Barry Buzan's work, and social constructivism, which is drawn upon by Tim Dunne.[19] These theories had a quite different orientation to the interpretivism of the early ES, focused as they all are on what Kenneth Waltz famously called the 'third image' of international relations (the international system) rather than the 'first image' (the individual actor).[20]

Of course, these moves – the turns to critical theory and to alternative explanatory theories – have not disadvantaged the ES in the broader marketplace of ideas in IR, nor have they prevented the production of excellent work by scholars committed to it. The recent publication of an International Studies Association *Guide to the English School* (2013) is testimony to the success of the new ES; the production of excellent books and articles, especially on historical and non-Western international societies, continues unabated.[21] But they do diverge in approach from that of the interpretive orientation of the early ES.

Given all that the new ES has achieved, it could be argued that the abandonment of the interpretivism of the early ES has paid dividends. But as Buzan notes in his recent overview of the School, it continues to be dogged by the criticism that it is complacent or even sloppy when it comes to matters of method.[22] To gain clarity, it may therefore be helpful to distinguish between different approaches taken by different parts of the ES, rather than arguing that the School as a whole embraces methodological pluralism, as some have suggested.[23] On the one hand, there is the approach of the early ES which insists that social behaviour can only be explained by reference to the meanings those actions have for those who perform them, and that this is done by interpreting the interpretations of the social world held by agents.[24] On the other, there are the various approaches of the later ES, who maintain that social behaviour in international relations can be explained by focusing not on the first image but on the third, on the ideational and material structures of international society, which the later ES thinks determines or at least constrains the behaviour of individual actors.[25]

Notes

1. I am very grateful to Robert Murray for his invitation to contribute this chapter and his comments on earlier drafts.

2. On this phase, see especially Brunello Vigezzi, *The British Committee and the Theory of International Politics (1954–1985): The Rediscovery of History* (Milan: Edizione Unicopli, 2005); and Tim Dunne, *Inventing International Society: A History of the English School* (Basingstoke: Macmillan, 1998).

3. See, for example, the contrast – made by Roy Jones in the article named 'The English School' – between Charles Manning's approach, shaped by idealist metaphysics, and Martin Wight's, shaped by historical modes of thinking derived from Herbert Butterfield, Arnold J. Toynbee and others. See Roy Jones, 'The English School of International Relations: A Case for Closure', *Review of International Studies* 7:1 (1981), 1-13.

4. On interpretivism in the social sciences, see especially Mark Bevir and R. A. W. Rhodes, 'Defending Interpretation', *European Political Science* 5 (2006): 69-83; and for a critique, see Colin Hay, 'Interpreting Interpretivism Interpreting Interpretations: The New Hermeneutics of Public Administration', *Public Administration* 89:1 (2011): 167-82.

5. Herbert Butterfield and Martin Wight, 'Preface', in *Diplomatic Investigations: Essays on the Theory of International Politics*, eds Herbert Butterfield and Martin Wight (London: Allen & Unwin, 1966), 12.

6. Ibid., 12-13.

7. Ibid., 13.

8. Coral Bell, 'The United Nations and the West', *International Affairs* 29:4 (1953), 464-72; Coral Bell, *Negotiation from Strength: A Study in the Politics of Power* (London: Chatto & Windus, 1962); Peter Lyon, *Neutralism* (Leicester: Leicester University Press, 1963); Herbert Butterfield, *International Conflict in the Twentieth Century: A Christian View* (London: Routledge & Kegan Paul, 1960); Martin Wight, 'The Balance of Power', in *Survey of International Affairs: The World in March 1939*, eds Arnold J. Toynbee and F. T. Ashton-Gwatkin (London: Oxford University Press, 1952), 508-31, Martin Wight, 'The Power Balance at the United Nations', Proceedings of the Institute of World Affairs, 33rd session (Los Angeles, CA: University of Southern California), 247-59; and Martin Wight, *International Theory: The Three Traditions*, eds Brian Porter and Gabriele Wight (Leicester: Leicester University Press, 1990).

9. The case for using interpretivism in international relations is put well by Mark Neufeld in 'Interpretation and the 'Science' of International Relations', *Review of International Studies* 19 (1993), 39-61.

10. Hedley Bull, 'The Grotian Conception of International Society', in *Diplomatic Investigations*, eds Butterfield and Wight, 51.

11. Herbert Butterfield, 'The Balance of Power', in *Diplomatic Investigations*, eds Butterfield and Wight, 132-148.

12. Ibid., 147.

13. See especially Martin Wight, 'Western Values in International Relations', in *Diplomatic Investigations*, eds Butterfield and Wight, 89-90.

14. Roger Epp, 'The English School on the Frontiers of International Society: A Hermeneutic Recollection', *Review of International Studies* 24 (1998) (Special Issue), 49-51.

15. Ibid., 55.

16. This is not to say, however, that it completely disappeared or that it did not have powerful and influential exponents. See especially Charles Taylor, 'Interpretation and the Sciences of Man', *The Review of Metaphysics* 25:1 (1971): 3-51.

17. See, for example, Michael Donelan, ed., *The Reason of States* (London: Allen and Unwin, 1978); Murray Forsyth, *Unions of States: The Theory and Practice of Confederation* (Leicester: Leicester University Press, 1981); Alan James, *Sovereign Statehood: The Basis of International Society* (London: Allen and Unwin, 1986); James Mayall, *The Community of States* (London: Allen and Unwin, 1982); James Mayall, *Nationalism and International Society* (Cambridge: Cambridge University Press, 1990); Cornelia Navari, *The Condition of States* (Buckingham: Open University Press, 1991); R. J. Vincent, *Nonintervention and International Order* (Princeton, NJ: Princeton University Press, 1974); and R. J. Vincent, *Human Rights and International Relations* (Cambridge: Cambridge University Press, 1986).

18. See especially Andrew Linklater, 'Men and Citizens in International Relations', *Review of International Relations* 7:1 (1981), 23-37, as well as *Men and Citizens in the Theory of International Relations*, 2nd ed. (Basingstoke: Macmillan, 1990) and *The Transformation of Political Community: Ethical Foundations of the Post-Westphalian Era* (Cambridge: Polity, 1998). For Linklater's views on the ES, see Andrew Linklater and Hidemi Suganami, *The English School of International Relations: A Contemporary Reassessment* (Cambridge: Cambridge University Press, 2006).

19. See Hedley Bull, *The Anarchical Society: A Study of Order in World Politics*, 1st ed. (London: Macmillan, 1977); Barry Buzan, 'From International System to International Society: Structural Realism and Regime Theory Meet the English School', *International Organization* 47:3 (1993), 327-52; Tim Dunne, 'The Social Construction of International Society', *European Journal of International Relations* 1:3 (1995), 367-89.

20. Kenneth N. Waltz, *Man, the State, and War: A Theoretical Analysis* (New York: Columbia University Press, 1959).

21. Daniel Green and Cornelia Navari, eds, *Guide to the English School of International Studies* (London: John Wiley & Sons, 2013). See also, *inter alia*, Barry Buzan and Ana Gonzalez-Perez, eds, *International Society and the Middle East: English School Theory at the Regional Level* (Basingstoke: Macmillan, 2009) and Barry Buzan and Yongjin Zhang, eds, *Contesting International Society in East Asia* (Cambridge: Cambridge University Press, 2014).

22. Barry Buzan, *An Introduction to the English School of International Relations: The Societal Approach* (Cambridge: Polity, 2014), 170-71.

23. Richard Little, 'The English School's Contribution to Study of International Relations', *European Journal of International Relations* 6:3 (2000): 395-422.

24. On this point, see also Cornelia Navari, 'The Concept of Practice in the English School', *European Journal of International Relations* 17:4 (2011): 611-30.

25. The best expression of this approach is Barry Buzan, *From International to World Society? English School Theory and the Social Structure of Globalisation* (Cambridge: Cambridge University Press, 2004). For a much more thorough exploration of ES methods than is provided here, see also the various essays in Cornelia Navari, ed., *Theorising International Society: English School Methods* (Basingstoke: Palgrave, 2009).

5

Civilisations and International Society

ANDREW LINKLATER
ABERYSTWYTH UNIVERSITY, UK

Interest in civilisations has increased in recent years, as the recent publication of Peter Katzenstein's three edited volumes reveals.[1] As with Huntington's discussion of the clash of civilisations, most of the literature has dealt – but not explicitly – with what Hedley Bull and Adam Watson, in one of the pioneering works of the English School, called 'the expansion of international society'.[2] The driving idea behind that book was that international society has outgrown Europe, the region in which the society of states and its core institutions such as permanent diplomacy and international law first developed. It is important to note the importance of a central theme in Wight's reflections on different state-systems. All of them – the Hellenic, ancient Chinese, and modern European – had emerged, he argued, in a region where there was a keen awareness of a shared civilisational identity. The corollary was a powerful sense of 'cultural differentiation' from the supposedly 'savage' or 'barbaric' world.[3]

Wight's position was that the members of states-systems found it easier to agree on common institutions and values because they were part of the same civilisation. They inherited certain concepts and sensibilities from the distant past that enabled them to introduce elements of civility into the context of anarchy – to establish what Bull in his most famous work called 'the anarchical society'.[4] The sense of belonging to one civilisation made it possible for the societies involved to place some restraints on the use of force – at least in their relations with each other. The idea of civilisation had rather different consequences as far as relations with the outlying 'barbaric' world were concerned. European colonial wars revealed that the 'civilised' did not believe they should observe the same restraints in their conflicts with 'savages'. The latter were not protected by the laws of war. They could not be expected, so it was supposed, to observe the principles of reciprocity that were valued in the 'civilised world. Parallels are evident in the recent language that was used as part of the 'war on terror' to describe the members of 'uncivilised' terrorist groups – the so-called 'unlawful combatants'.

That example indicates that the language of civilisation and barbarism is no longer merely of historical interest. But to return to an earlier theme, its continuing political salience is a function of the challenges that have resulted from the expansion of international society. Before the twentieth century, the European empires denied that their colonies could belong to international society as equals. The establishment of the League of Nations Mandate System, followed by the United Nations Trusteeship System, held out the prospect of eventual membership of international society.[5]

But at the time, most thought that the colonies in Africa, Asia and the Pacific would need many decades, if not centuries, to learn to stand on their feet as independent members of international society. They would first have to 'modernise' after the fashion of the dominant European or Western states. That orientation to the non-Western world reflected the influence of the nineteenth-century 'standard of civilisation'. The concept referred to the idea that only the civilised, as Europeans understood the term, could belong to the society of states. As for the others, they could at least be made aware of the standards by which they were judged, and they could comprehend how they would have to change before they could be admitted to international society. Similar ideas were held to apply to societies such as Japan and China that were regarded as 'advanced' but also less 'civilised' than the Europeans. Demonstrating their willingness and ability to conform to Western principles of international relations was essential before any claim to gain entry to international society could be considered.[6]

It is worth noting that references to civilisation were widespread in international legal discussions of the laws of war in the late nineteenth and early twentieth centuries.[7] In a similar fashion, the idea of civilisation was invoked by the prosecutors in the Nuremberg and Tokyo war crimes tribunals. But that language is not used so overtly today. References to the differences between one's own 'civilised' ways and others' 'savage' practices attract condemnation. That is an indication of significant changes in 'post-imperial' international society. It was once perfectly legitimate – so the Europeans believed – to use a language that is now a sharp, and embarrassing, reminder of the discredited colonial age.

Not that all of the sensibilities that informed the standard of civilisation have departed the scene. Recent literature has discussed the ways in which the human rights culture rests on a new standard of civilisation; similar claims have been made with respect to market society and liberal democracy.[8] Those discussions stress that international society is far from 'post-European' or 'post-Western' in terms of its organising principles and core practices. They draw attention to the respects in which international society has yet to ensure cultural justice for non-European peoples, a point that was stressed in Bull's writings on the 'revolt against the West' and in Keal's discussion of how the continuing marginalisation of indigenous peoples is testimony to the 'moral backwardness of international society.'[9]

Such explorations demonstrate that the principles of international relations that developed in one civilisation – Europe – continue to shape contemporary world politics. They suggest that international society has outgrown Europe but it has not exactly outgrown European or Western civilisation. Its dominance has meant that the most powerful societies have not come under sustained pressure to construct an international society that does justice to different cultures or civilisations.[10]

Complex questions arise about the social-scientific utility of notions of civilisation, but they cannot be considered in this chapter. It is perhaps best to think less in terms of civilisations and more about civilising processes – the processes by which different peoples, and not only the Europeans, came to regard their practices as civilised and to regard others as embodying the barbarism they thought they had left behind. Major studies of how Europeans came to think of themselves as civilised can be found in the sociological literature.[11] Their importance for students of international society has been discussed in recent work.[12] But too little is known in the West about non-European civilising processes, and about their impact on European civilisation over the last few centuries.[13] Related problems arise in connection with what are sometimes dismissed as 'pre-modern' responses to Western 'modernity'. They need to be understood not as a revolt against the West by peoples who have supposedly failed to adapt to modernity but, more sympathetically, as diverse responses to profound economic, political and cultural dislocations – and reactions to the complex interweaving of Western and non-Western influences – that are part of the legacy of Western imperialism.[14]

Such inquiries will become ever more important as new centres of power develop outside the West. The idea of civilisation may have lost its importance as a binding force in international society, but understanding different, but interwoven civilising processes, is critical for promoting mutual respect and trust between the diverse peoples that have been forced together over the last few centuries, and who comprise international society today.

Notes

1. Peter J. Katzenstein, ed., *Civilizations in World Politics: Plural and Pluralist Perspectives* (Abingdon: Routledge, 2010); Peter J. Katzenstein, ed., *Sinicazation and the Rise of China: Civilizational Processes Beyond East and West* (Abingdon: Routledge, 2012); Peter J. Katzenstein, ed., *Anglo-America and its Discontents: Civilizational Identities Beyond West and East* (Abingdon: Routledge, 2012).

2. Samuel Huntington, *The Clash of Civilizations and the Remaking of World Order* (Simon and Schuster: New York, 1996); Hedley Bull and Adam Watson, eds, *The Expansion of International Society* (Clarendon Press: Oxford, 1984).

3. Martin Wight, *Systems of States* (Leicester: Leicester University Press, 1979), ch. 1.

4. Hedley Bull, *The Anarchical Society: A Study of Order in World Politics* (London, Macmillan, 1977).

5. William Bain, *Between Anarchy and Society: Trusteeship and the Obligations of Power* (Oxford: Oxford University Press, 2003).

6. Gerrit Gong, *The Standard of 'Civilisation' in International Society* (Oxford: Clarendon Press, 1984); Shogo Suzuki, *Civilization and Empire. China and Japan's Encounter with European International Society* (Abingdon: Routledge, 2009); Shogo Suzuki, 'Viewing the Development of Human Society from Asia', *Human Figurations: Long-Term Perspectives on the Human Condition*, 1:2 (2012), http://www.norberteliasfoundation.nl (accessed January 23, 2013).

7. Martti Koskenniemi, *The Gentle Civilizer of Nations: The Rise and Fall of International Law, 1870-1960* (Cambridge: Cambridge University Press, 2001).

8. Jack Donnelly, 'Human Rights: A New Standard of Civilization?' *International Affairs* 74:1 (1998), 1-23; Brett Bowden and Leonard Seabrooke, eds, *Global Standards of Market Civilization* (Abingdon: Routledge, 2006); Christopher Hobson, 'Democracy as Civilization', *Global Society* 22:1 (2008), 75-95.

9. Hedley Bull, 'Justice in International Relations', *The Hagey Lectures* (Ontario: University of Waterloo, 1984), reprinted in K. Alderson and A. Hurrell, eds, *Hedley Bull on International Society* (London: Macmillan, 2000); Paul Keal, *European Conquest and the Rights of Indigenous Peoples: The Moral Backwardness of International Society* (Cambridge: Cambridge University Press, 2003).

10. Richard Shapcott, *Justice, Community and Dialogue in International Relations* (Cambridge: Cambridge University Press, 2001).

11. Norbert Elias, *On the Process of Civilisation: Sociogenetic and Psychogenetic Investigations* (Dublin: University College Dublin Press, [1939] 2012).

12. Andrew Linklater, *The Problem of Harm in World Politics: Theoretical Investigations* (Cambridge: Cambridge University Press, 2011); John M. Hobson, *The Eurocentric Conception of World Politics: Western International Theory, 1760-2010* (Cambridge, Cambridge University Press, 2012).

13. Stephen Mennell, 'Asian and European Civilizing Processes Compared', in *The Course of Human History: Economic Growth, Social Process, and Civilization*, eds J. Goudsblom, E. Jones and S. Mennell (London: M. E. Sharpe, 1996); John M. Hobson, *The Eastern Origins of Western Civilization* (Cambridge: Cambridge University Press, 2004).

14. Pankaj Mishra, *From the Ruins of Empire: The Revolt against the West and the Remaking of Empire* (London: Allen Lane, 2012); Mustapha Pasha, 'Islam, Soft Orientalism and Empire: A Gramscian Rereading', in *Gramsci, Political Economy and*

International Relations Theory: Modern Princes and Naked Emperors, ed. A. Ayers (Basingstoke: Palgrave, 2008); Mustapha Pasha, 'Global Exception and Islamic Exceptionalism', *International Politics*, 46:5 (2009); Mustapha Pasha, 'Global Leadership and the Islamic World: Crisis, Contention and Challenge', in *Global Crises and the Crisis of Global Leadership*, ed. S. Gill (Cambridge: Cambridge University Press, 2012).

6

Translation and Interpretation: The English School and IR Theory in China

ROGER EPP

UNIVERSITY OF ALBERTA, CANADA

In a recent article in the *Review of International Studies*, Zhang Xiaoming identifies what he calls the English School's theoretical 'inventions' of China.[1] On one hand, he notes, Martin Wight, Hedley Bull and the British Committee in which they were active participants showed a serious, historical interest in China at a time when the field of international relations typically did not. China figured in their explorations of comparative state-systems, standards of civilisations, and the so-called revolt against the West. Wight's undergraduate lectures introduced traditions of classical Chinese thought in parallel with European traditions on the question of the barbarian. Bull, indeed, travelled to China for three weeks in 1973. But on the other hand, Zhang argues, these engagements are marked by selectivity and ethnocentrism. The story they tell is a European one, with China the outsider, sometimes the provocateur. The effect, he concludes, is to limit the English School's appeal relative to other imported theoretical positions.

My purpose in this short chapter is neither to correct Professor Zhang's careful reading nor to defend the English School – a 'brand' about which I have my own doubts – as a universal project. Rather, in response, it is to make a more modest case for an interpretive mode of theorising,[2] one that begins by embracing Professor Zhang's point: 'Every IR theory is provincial in cultural terms'.[3] Interpretive theory pays attention to history, words, meanings and translations; it risks honest encounters with what it is unfamiliar; and it is willing to rethink its own certainties on the basis of those encounters. It does not assume incommensurability. It asks instead what interpretive resources –

what bridges – might be present within a theoretical tradition to enable a fuller understanding. Needless to say, this orientation stands outside the mainstream. At a time when IR has become established at universities around world, its theoretical literature nonetheless is still overwhelmingly parochial and positivist. As one sobering new study has shown, the reading lists that form the next professorial generation at leading graduate programmes in the United States and Europe consist almost entirely of the conventional Western canon.[4] Whether that canon's endurance is proof of its scientific validity, intellectual hegemony or timidity, the result is a discipline 'rooted in a rather narrow and particular historical experience' and hard-pressed to envision a 'future outside of the Westphalian box'.[5]

In China, where IR has emerged from the practical imperatives of ideology and foreign policy, there is no shortage of theoretical activity.[6] Some of it is done uncritically within imported templates – aided by doctoral educations overseas and a continuing airlift of professors and texts in translation from the US. But China, as one scholar has put it, is now 'between copying and constructing'.[7] Increasingly, theory in the social sciences is assumed to have a geocultural dimension. Scholars have turned to their own civilisational sources, whether it is Confucius and other classical thinkers on humane statecraft in the Warring States period[8]; the imperial tributary model and the corresponding world-order concepts of *tianxia* (all-under-heaven) and *datong* (harmony)[9]; or else the more recent experience of colonial humiliation, revolution, outsider status and 'peaceful rise'. The quest for IR theory with Chinese cultural characteristics is meant typically not as a hermetic enterprise but as a step towards engagement with other scholars.[10]

The English School is well placed to take up this conversation, I think, so long as it is clear about its purposes. If its influence in China a decade ago was 'marginal',[11] it has now acquired a modest following, for reasons that include its humanistic and historicist orientation, its value as a counterweight and, not least, its implicit encouragement of a parallel 'Chinese School'.[12] Select texts like Bull's *The Anarchical Society* are available in translation. But there is something at stake in China other than market share and brand penetration. China represents a practical test of the commitment to interpretive inquiry. It will not flatten easily into the realist shorthand of national interest or the liberal teleology of peace through cultural–commercial convergence. Its scholars ought to be engaged, not with offers of inclusion in the 'expansion' of academic IR, not with a theory of the whole, not with a rigid or exoticised assumption of civilisational difference, but out of a respectful need for interpreters, translators and collaborators in understanding a complex world – one in which the West is no longer comfortably at the centre.

Wight's work will be particularly helpful in this respect. His published lectures and the essays in *Systems of States* treat the modern state-system as a historical-linguistic artefact, born of a 'peculiar' *European* culture. He provincialises international society.[13] He delimits its ethical experience in terms of 'Western values.'[14] But, equally, he explores its outer limits, spatial and temporal, how it reveals itself, how it is constituted by what happens on its frontiers. He traces the emergence of the idea of Europe against the spectre of the Turk and of modern international law through the sixteenth-century Spanish encounter with the indigenous inhabitants of the Americas: were they fully human, were they peoples, and, if yes, what was owed them? His lectures on the barbarian keep the memory within IR of colonial atrocities, political exclusions, dispossessions by force and by law, and, a century ago, tutelary rationalisations of empire.[15] If Wight's inquiries are ethnocentric, they are not uncritical. Invariably, they think through an encounter from one side of it, but they do not leave that side untouched; for in any such account it is the West – many 'Wests' – that must also be interrogated. What accounts for the periodic 'fits of world-conquering fanaticism?'[16]

It would be disingenuous for me to prescribe an IR theory with Chinese characteristics. At most, it is possible to say what a cross-cultural theoretical encounter might require: namely, risk, dialogue, attentiveness and introspection. In this sense, interpretive ways of thinking might be said to mirror the communicative practices of international diplomacy. They involve a double movement, towards the unfamiliar and then the familiar, describing and re-describing, rethinking that which had once seemed obvious. They show how much hinges on words, translations, gestures and protocols. The dialogue, in fact, may be 'uneasy'.[17] But Western scholars orientated to history, language and culture ought to be fascinated by the lead taken by their Chinese counterparts, for example, in rethinking conceptions of roles, rules, and relations,[18] or territoriality; or in excavating the range of meanings of *tianxia* and its possibilities for shaping a different global or regional order. They will wonder – this is the risk of the question – how contemporary China too reveals itself and is constituted by what happens on its edges, its frontiers, an insight that seems consonant with the classical sources on which those IR theorists have begun to draw; and then whether *tianxia* necessarily stands in contradiction with the insistence in Chinese policy on state sovereignty and territorial integrity, whether the former, hierarchical rather than horizontal, is, in fact, more deeply rooted culturally than the latter, and whether it should be regarded as pacific or aggressive.[19] The answer will require, *inter alia*, an account of how the word sovereignty itself is rendered in a language into which it once had to be translated and made intelligible. In the process, IR's 'universal' – for surely we all know what sovereignty is – will have been historicised and resituated on all sides with distinct cultural-linguistic nuances. Even sovereignty will not be the same.[20]

Which is why IR theory in the West, parochial and stale, may need Chinese scholarship at least as much as the reverse is true.

Notes

1. Zhang Xiaoming, 'China in the conception of international society: the English School's engagements with China', *Review of International Studies* 37 (2011): 763-86. I am grateful to Professor Zhang for the opportunity to present some of the ideas at a graduate seminar at the School of International Studies, Peking University, in October 2012.
2. Roger Epp, 'The English School on the frontiers of international society', *Review of International Studies* 24 (December 1998, Special Issue: The Eighty Years' Crisis, 1919–1999), 47-63.
3. Xiaoming, 'China in the conception of international society', 785.
4. Jonas Hagmann and Thomas J. Biersteker, 'Beyond the published discipline: toward a critical pedagogy of international studies', *European Journal of International Relations* 20 (2014): 291-315.
5. Amitav Acharya and Barry Buzan, 'Preface: Why is there no non-Western IR theory: reflections on and from Asia', *International Relations of the Asia-Pacific* 7 (2007): 285-86.
6. Zhang Yongjin, 'The 'English School' in China: a travelogue of ideas and their diffusion', *European Journal of International Relations* 9 (2003): 87-114, including an account of systematic US influence starting in the 1980s at pp. 101-103. See also, e.g., Qin Yaqing, 'Development of international relations theory in China: progress through debates', *International Relations of the Asia-Pacific* 11 (2011): 231-57; Ren Xiao, 'Toward a Chinese School of International Relations?' in *China and the New International Order*, eds Wang Gungwu and Zheng Yongnian (London: Routledge, 2008); Qin Yaqing, 'Why is there no Chinese international relations theory?', *International Relations of the Asia-Pacific* 7 (2007): 313-40; Gustaaf Geeraerts and Men Jing, 'International relations theory in China', *Global Society* 15 (2001): 251-76; and Song Xinning, 'Building international relations theory with Chinese characteristics', *Journal of Contemporary China* 10 (2001): 61-74.
7. Wang Yiwei, 'China: Between Copying and Constructing', in *International Relations Scholarship Around the World*, eds Arlene Tickner and Ole Wæver (London: Routledge, 2009).
8. See such diverse texts as Yan Xuetong, *Ancient Chinese Thought, Modern Chinese Power*, eds Daniel Bell and Sun Zhe, trans. Edmund Ryden (Princeton: Princeton University Press, 2011); Gustaaf Geeraerts and Men Jing, 'International relations theory in China'; Joseph Chan, 'Territorial Boundaries and Confucianism', and Ni Lixiong, 'The Implications of Ancient Chinese Military Culture for World Peace', in *Confucian Political Ethics*, ed. Daniel Bell (Princeton: Princeton University Press, 2008); Hsu Cho-Yun, 'Applying Confucian ethics to international relations', *Ethics and International Affairs* 5 (1991): 148-69.
9. For example, Zhao Tingyang, 'Rethinking empire from a Chinese concept, 'All-Under-Heaven' (*Tian-xia*)', *Social Identities* 12 (2006): 29-41; Yaqing, 'Chinese international relations theory?'; Shen Wenhua, 'Redefining Sovereignty', in *China and the New World Order*, eds Wang and Zheng; William Callahan, 'Chinese visions of

world order: post-hegemonic or a new hegemony?' *International Studies Review* 10 (2008): 749-61.

10. Wang Gungwu and Zheng Yongnian, 'Introduction', *China and the New International Order*, 17; Zhang Xiaoming, 'China in the conception of international society', 786.

11. Zhang Yongjin, 'The 'English School' in China: A Travelogue of Ideas and their Diffusion', 98.

12. See, e.g., Zhang Yongjin, 'A Travelogue of Ideas', 99-101; Ren Xiao, 'Toward a Chinese School of International Relations?' 297; Muthiah Alagappa, 'International relations studies in Asia: divergent trajectories', *International Relations of the Asia-Pacific* 11 (2011): 211; and Wang Jiangli and Barry Buzan, 'The English and Chinese schools of international relations: comparisons and lessons', *Chinese Journal of International Politics* 7 (2014): 1-46.

13. In this claim I am deliberately gesturing towards the work of Dipesh Chakrabarty, *Provincializing Europe: Postcolonial Thought and Historical Difference*, rev. ed. (Princeton: Princeton University Press, 2007).

14. Martin Wight, 'Western Values in International Relations', in *Diplomatic Investigations*, eds Herbert Butterfield and Martin Wight (London: George Allen and Unwin, 1966).

15. Martin Wight, *Systems of States*, ed. Hedley Bull (Leicester: Leicester University Press, 1977); Gabriele Wight and Brian Porter, eds, *International Theory: The Three Traditions* (Leicester: Leicester University Press/Royal Institute of International Affairs), ch. 4. I have relied on Wight's openings to think – in North America – about the presence and absence of aboriginal peoples in international theory. See 'At the Wood's Edge: Toward a Theoretical Clearing for Indigenous Diplomacies in International Relations', in *International Relations: Still an American Social Science?* eds Robert Crawford and Darryl Jarvis (Albany: State University of New York Press, 2001).

16. Wight, *International Theory*, 68.

17. Gustaaf Geeraerts and Men Jing, 'International relations theory in China', 251.

18. See, e.g., Qin Yaqing. 'Rule, rules and relations: towards a synthetic approach to governance', *Chinese Journal of International Politics* 4 (2011): 117-45.

19. While he is critical of Wight and the English School, William Callahan is a fine exemplar of the approach I have described. In addition to 'Chinese Visions of World Order', see his *Contingent States: Greater China and Transnational Relations* (Minneapolis: University of Minnesota Press, 2004), and *China: The Pessoptimist Nation* (Oxford: Oxford University Press, 2010).

20. Dipesh Chakrabarty's *Provincializing Europe* is a helpful text in framing the kind of translational theoretical encounter I imagine here.

7

An Overview of the English School's Engagement with Human Rights

ADRIAN GALLAGHER
UNIVERSITY OF LEEDS, UK

Students are often told that to study International Relations (IR) is to investigate relations *between* rather than *within* states. This is perhaps most often heard when critics of IR construct a 'straw-man' representation of the discipline which allows them to dismiss IR as too narrow. In other words, IR is said to be detached from the complexities of a twenty-first-century globalised world that demands students understand interconnected processes at the sub-national, national, and international level. The purpose of this piece, however, is to highlight that if one 'looks inside' IR one finds a much more diverse and enriching discipline. To do this, I focus on the English School's (ES) engagement with human rights to highlight that the ES has a strong tradition of concern regarding rights and responsibilities which stems from their world view that mass human rights violations within states are a matter of international concern.[1]

It is easy to understand why critics hold the view that state-centric approaches such as the ES do not accurately capture human relations from the local to the global level.[2] Indeed, one of the founding fathers of what came to be known as the ES,[3] Martin Wight, acknowledged that the study of international society concealed 'the *real* society of men and women'.[4] The statement clearly demonstrates that Wight was all too aware that the complex relations between citizens and states were an overlooked and under researched issue in IR. The ES 'top down' focus was then seemingly cemented in Hedley Bull's seminal study *The Anarchical Society* which offered an even more state-centric interpretation of international society than

Wight had originally envisaged.[5]   Published at the height of the Cold War, Bull's analysis represents a well documented trade-off between justice and order in which Bull prioritised the moral value of order over the moral pursuit of a just cause. From a contemporary perspective, this became the *pluralist position* in the ES with scholars such as James Mayall and Robert Jackson upholding the norm of non-intervention.[6]

A counter-development emerged in the 1980s. Bull's pluralist position changed as he argued that the consensus against Apartheid in South Africa should be used to mobilise international action against the human rights violations taking place.[7]   Expanding this understanding, R.J. Vincent's seminal study *Human Rights in International Relations* laid the foundation for what is currently referred to as the ES *solidarist position* as he argued that basic human rights should be understood as floor beneath states rather than a ceiling above them.[8] In other words, even without a world government, political elites should abide by a universal moral minimalism. As contemporary scholars both inside and outside the ES have acknowledged, Vincent's work does not just stand as one of the first studies on human rights from an IR perspective but more importantly acted to rehabilitate 'serious theoretical discussion on human rights in general.'[9] In the post-Cold War era, Tim Dunne and Nicholas Wheeler expanded this solidarist doctrine and in so doing, stood at the forefront of humanitarian intervention debate.[10] More recently, the solidarist baton has been passed on to Alex Bellamy, who works within an ES framework while producing cutting-edge research on the Responsibility to Protect (R2P).[11] At the same time, Dunne acted as director of research at the Asia Centre for the Responsibility to Protect.[12] Accordingly, this historical trajectory helps illustrate that ES has played a pivotal role in shaping contemporary understandings of human rights and continues to do so.

With much ink spilt elsewhere on the division between the pluralist-solidarist divide outlined in the two different ES strands above, this author would like to raise a final point on the ES's potential contribution to a new research agenda. In William Bain's analysis of Nicholas Wheeler's decisive, *Saving Strangers*, he claims, 'it seems as though Wheeler merely invokes humanity as a self-evident moral truth – the authority of which requires no further explanation – which in the end cannot tell us the reasons why we should act to save strangers.'[13] The statement draws attention to a problem that the ES has an under-theorised understanding of humanity which in turn fails to explain why 'we' should act to save 'them'. One response is to forge a better understanding of the relationship between the society of states and humanity which addresses the relationship between the ES and cosmopolitanism. Andrew Linklater has stood at the forefront of this research for over two decades.[14] Alternatively, ES scholars could focus on the concept of order, rather than humanity, to investigate the impact that mass human rights violations have on the ordering principles of international society. It is this latter research agenda that I develop in *Genocide and Its Threat to Contemporary International Order*.[15] This is not to say that this latter focus is mutually exclusive from the former, but that these are two timely and important research agendas which ES scholars can make a significant contribution towards in the future.[16]

In summary, IR is often presented as somewhat of an ill, dying discipline that will fade away as it fails to explain and understand the complexities of the twenty-first century. Yet when one looks at the most important issues in contemporary international politics, the crises in Syria, Libya, Yemen, and Mali to name just a few, it is evident that although the ES does not explain everything it does provides a fruitful framework for analysing the optimism and tragedy that lies at the heart of international society. After all, the ES view remains that 'there is more to international relations than the realist suggests but less than the cosmopolitan desires.'[17]

Notes

1.   In relation to globalization and the ES, see Barry Buzan, *From International Society to World Society? English School Theory and the Social Structure of Globalisation* (Cambridge: Cambridge University Press, 2006).

2.   Martin Shaw, *Global Society and International Relations, Sociological Concepts and Political Perspectives* (Cambridge: Polity Press, 1994), ch. 5. Also, Richard Falk, *Achieving Human Rights* (London: Routledge, 2009), 17.

3.   Roy Jones, 'The English School of International Relations: A Case for Closure', *Review of International Studies* 7:1 (1981) 1-13.

4.   Martin Wight, 'Western Values in International Relations', in *Diplomatic Investigations: Essays in the Theory of International Politics,* eds Herbert Butterfield and Martin Wight (London: Allen and Unwin, 1966), 93.

5.   Hedley Bull, *The Anarchical Society, A Study of World Order Politics*, 3rd ed. (London: Palgrave, 2002).

6.   James Mayall, *World Politics: Progress and its Limits* (Cambridge: Polity, 2000); Robert Jackson, *The Global Covenant, Human Conduct in a World of States* (Oxford: Oxford University Press, 2000).

7.   Hedley Bull, 'The West and South Africa', *Daedalus* 111:2 (1982), 266.

8.   Raymond. J., Vincent, *Human Rights in International Relations* (London: Cambridge University Press, 1986), 126.

9.   Nicholas J. Rengger, 'The World Turned Upside Down? Human Rights and International Relations after 25 years', *International Affairs* 87:5 (2011), 1160.

10.   Nicholas J. Wheeler, *Saving Strangers: Humanitarian Intervention in International Society* (Oxford: Oxford University Press, 2000).

11.   Alex J. Bellamy, 'Humanitarian Intervention and the Three Traditions', *Global Society* 17:1 (2003), 3-20; Alex J. Bellamy, *Global Politics and The Responsibility to Protect*

(New York: Routledge, 2011).

12. Asia Centre for the Responsibility to Protect, http://www.r2pasiapacific.org/ (accessed February 26, 2013).

13. William Bain, 'One Order, Two Laws: Recovering the "Normative" in English School Theory', *Review of International Studies* 33:4 (2007), 561.

14. For an overview see Andrew Linklater, *Critical Theory and World Politics: Citizenship, Sovereignty and Humanity* (New York: Routledge: 2007). Also, his ongoing three-volume study on harm, Andrew Linklater, *The Problem of Harm in World Politics* (New York, Oxford University Press, 2011).

15. Adrian Gallagher, *Genocide and Its Threat to Contemporary International Order* (Basingstoke: Palgrave Macmillan, 2013).

16. Professor Jason Ralph and I are currently supervising PhDs in the Department of Politics and International Studies at the University of Leeds related to these research agendas.

17. Andrew Linklater, 'Rationalism' in Scott Burchill, Andrew Linklater, Richard Devetak, Jack Donnelly, Terry Nardin, Matthew Paterson, Christian Reus-Smit, and Jaqui True, *Theories of International Relation*, 4th ed. (London: Palgrave Macmillan, 1996), 95.

8

Moral Responsibility in International Relations: The US Response to Rwanda

CATHINKA VIK

GJØVIK UNIVERSITY COLLEGE, NORWAY

The English School offers an account of international relations that captures the interplay between morality and power; the empirical and the normative; the pluralist and the solidarist; order and justice; theory and history.[1] It thus provides a holistic framework for analysing the central question to any normative theory, namely the moral value to be attributed to particularistic political collectivities against humanity taken as a whole, or the claims of individual human beings. This question remains at the heart of international relations as one the most challenging moral questions of our time.

The international community has in recent decades made great strides in a solidarist direction.[2] Corroborating the conditionality of state sovereignty, it is now widely accepted that there exists some sort of collective moral 'responsibility to protect' in situations where the state fails in its obligation to protect its own people. In accordance with this development, the question has emerged as to whether the expanded notion of moral responsibility animating the responsibility to protect is becoming solidified as an actionable norm in international relations.

Yet, despite this promising development, we continue to witness inconsistent responses to massive human rights violations across the globe. One of the reasons for this failure – and one that is commonly neglected in discussions about humanitarian interventions – is the primary moral duty of the government of potential intervening countries to their own citizens and the dilemma this creates for the consistent implementation of the nascent R2P norm.

According to the United Nations Charter, the primary responsibility for the maintenance of international peace and security rests with the United Nations Security Council. With this, the international community has left the responsibility of protecting humanity's interests in the hands of state leaders elected to protect the lives and promote the interests of their respective populations. A problem thus emerges, as state leaders find themselves struggling to reconcile their pluralist (national) and solidarist (international) commitments. While there is universal agreement that, in the face of severe human rights violations, 'something must be done', the idea that states refusing to commit troops to end such atrocities are morally bereft is not axiomatic.[3] Charged with the primary responsibility of protecting national citizens and promoting their best interests, it is pertinent to question whether it is realistic to expect state leaders to make moral decisions independent of national interest when confronted with situations of severe human rights violations abroad.

When confronted with situations of severe human rights violations, therefore, the question is not only one of whether individual human rights or state sovereignty should take precedence in situations where a choice between the two has to be made, as it is often presented, but also one of how the decision to intervene/not intervene is justified to the citizens of the intervening country and whether the deployment of soldiers to protect nationals of a foreign country can be vindicated domestically. The twofold moral commitment to uphold human rights domestically and internationally often confronts state leaders with conflicting moral imperatives. It may not always be easy to assess which imperative should be followed. This is especially the case in prospective humanitarian interventions, where the outcome is so difficult to predict with any certainty. Striving to reconcile its domestic and international commitments, the state is thus engaged in a two-level game between domestic and international preferences, where power and morality is inextricably linked. This process is not static, but one in which discourse and action continuously shape the state as a moral actor, and our collective understanding of how and when power can be vindicated.

One of the dangers inherent in current approaches to the concept of moral responsibility in international politics is their tendency to collapse individual and state morality. Due to the moral complexity of statecraft, the moral stance of states and policy-makers must be separated from the moral stance of individuals. As famously suggested by Niccolo Machiavelli:

> It must be understood, however, that a prince [...] cannot observe all of those virtues for which men are reputed good, because it is often necessary to act against mercy, against faith, against humanity, against frankness, against religion in order to preserve the state. Thus he must be disposed to change according as the winds of fortune and the alternations of circumstance dictate. [...] he must stick to the good so long as he can, but being compelled by necessity, he must be ready to take the way of evil [...].[4]

Yet, this is not to suggest that the complexity of statecraft excuses inaction in response to situations of genocide. On the contrary, an international community serious about the pledge of 'never again' must address this complexity in order to avoid continued inconsistencies in response to mass atrocities. In order to secure consistent responses to situations of severe human rights violations, therefore, the unique ethical sphere of statecraft must be addressed.

By focusing on relations between and among entities rather than on the alleged dispositional qualities of static entities within a social context, relational constructivism is useful in analysing this dynamic process.[5] From this perspective, the practical activities implemented in response to mass atrocities continually produce and reproduce actors such as 'the state' and 'the international community' and their notion of moral responsibility in international relations, which again give rise to the observed social actions carried out in its name.[6] Activities devoted to legitimation are particularly interesting in this regard since these activities are among the clearest moments at which actors are produced in practice.[8] [8]

An English School analysis of the US response to the 1994 Rwandan genocide provides an illustrative example, suggesting that the government's dithering response was reflective of an attempt to act according to a pluralist understanding of international relations in a context challenging its limited notion of moral responsibility among states and individuals across political and cultural boundaries.

The genocide in Rwanda created an unprecedented opportunity for the United States to provide political and moral leadership in the development of a blueprint for post-Cold War collective security responses to mass atrocities. However, concerned that the declaration of 'genocide' would demand decisive action according to the UN Genocide Convention, the United States arguably led the international community in a rhetorical dance to avoid the term. Beyond the discursive efforts to undermine the situation in Rwanda in order to avoid expectations warranting undesirable action, the US lobbied for a total withdrawal of UN forces in Rwanda in April 1994. Domestic politics, dominated by democratic infighting; the legacy of Somalia;[9] and narrowly defined national interests produced consistent delays and impediments as hundreds of thousands were massacred under the Hutu extremists' genocidal assault.

Throughout his presidency, the Clinton administration arguably struggled to reconcile its expressed intent to support the solidarist values articulated in the UN Genocide Convention with its commitment to more pluralist principles of state sovereignty and non-intervention in other states' domestic affairs. This tension was reflected in the inconsistency with which the Clinton administration put the principles of humanitarian intervention into practice and the accompanying erratic justifications of these responses. Drawing on the ideological reservoir of the pluralist foreign policy tradition, the Clinton administration justified its inaction by referencing narrowly defined national interests, thus avoiding discourse that would have warranted intervention on humanitarian grounds.[10]

Yet the Rwandan case also reveals how this process of legitimation simultaneously changed public expectations of how the US should respond to similar situations in the future, thus shaping the identity of the state as a moral actor in international relations. Undermining the pluralist normative foundation of his own administration's practices during the 1994 'Clinton apology' by delegitimising the beliefs on which they were based, the president advanced the solidarist expanded notion of moral responsibility later articulated in R2P by attributing moral responsibility to the US to prevent or suppress similar situations of genocide and mass atrocity in the future.

The controversy surrounding the question of moral responsibility in international relations can thus be viewed as reflective of an international community striving to reconcile its pluralist and solidarist foundations. With the evolution of solidarism, new complexities associated with the concept of moral responsibility are revealed at the state level. The question we must ask ourselves is whether the complexity of considerations excuses inaction when confronted with situations of severe human rights violations. Despite the pledge of 'never again', we continue to accept excuses based on a pluralist limited understanding of moral responsibility to stand idly by while genocide unfolds. When is an excuse good enough that we consider it acceptable? How do we expect state leaders to balance different moral responsibilities in an increasingly interconnected global community? The English School account of power and morality; the empirical and the normative; the pluralist and solidarist; order and justice; theory and history, not as opposite positions, but rather as coexisting dimensions of an international order within which tensions arise,[11] provides a useful starting point for further exploration of these essential questions that are likely to remain among the most central questions of international politics in years to come.

Notes

1. Tim Dunne, 'The English School', *The Oxford Handbook of International Relations* (London: Sage Publications, 2008).
2. In the realms of social and political philosophy, cosmopolitanism is considered the idea that all human beings belong to a single moral community; one which exists regardless of social circumstances, and to which universal moral principles apply (Howard Fienberg, 'Morality Comes to IR: Ethical Approaches to the Discipline', http://www.hfienberg.com/irtheory/brown.html [accessed July 30, 2010]). The pluralist argument, in contrast, delineates the international scene into geographic communities, which formulate the individual's morality, in a social rather than natural context. For pluralists, the nation-state is considered a community whose members are bound by strong ties of solidarity from which moral feelings and a sense of ethical obligation naturally derive (Stanley Hoffman, *Duties Beyond Borders: On the Limits and Possibilities of Ethical International Politics* [New York: Syracuse University Press, 1981]). Pluralists thus appeal to particularistic foundations of morality, viewing the state as 'the framework that founds and enables the ethical discourse in which social judgments are possible' (Molly Cochran, 'Cosmopolitanism and Communitarianism in a Post-Cold War World', *Boundaries in Question: New Directions in International Relations* [London: Pinter, 1995], 48). In this view, without the existence of a higher authority analogous to the state, this framework does not exist at the international level.
3. Aidan Hehir, 'Political Will, Non-Intervention and the Responsibility to Protect', Presentation at the International Studies Association meeting, February 2011.
4. Niccolo Machiavelli, *The Prince*, trans. Daniel Donno (1984), 93.
5. Patrick Thaddeus Jackson, 'Relational Constructivism: A War of Words', *Making Sense of International Relations Theory* (London, UK: Lynne Rienner, 2006).
6. David Dessler, 'What's at Stake in the Agent-Structure Debate?' *International Organization* 43:3 (1989), 462.
7. Jackson, 'Relational Constructivism: A War of Words'.
8. This relational constructivist approach allows for the unpacking of concepts, such as what it means for the 'government' to 'act'. Action, from a relational perspective, is a matter of social attribution, as certain activities are encoded or characterised as the doings of some social actor. The social attribution simultaneously produces the actor as legitimately able to perform the action in question, and legitimises the action because this actor performs it. Legitimation processes isolate certain activities (i.e. responses to situations of severe human rights violations) and render them acceptable by characterising them as the activities of 'the state'. In doing so, they reproduce the state itself. It is in these boundary demarcations that 'the state' has its most tangible existence and its most concrete presence in the daily lives of those under its authority. The state is less the determinate origin of any given social action and more a product of the processes of legitimation that produce and sustain it in particular settings. Thus, the government's authority and responsibility has to be continually negotiated and

sustained in practice. Thinking of 'the international community', 'the UN Security Council' and 'the government' of the potential intervener in this way allows us to grasp the stakes of the justifications of responses to situations of severe human rights abuses waged by politicians and other officials.

The relational constructivist approach thus views statements as participants in an ongoing process of legitimation directed at humanitarian interventions. In this process, statements draw on rhetorical commonplaces already present in the social environment surrounding a particular incident (Friedrich Kratochwil, *Rules, Norms, and Decisions* [Cambridge: Cambridge University Press, 1989], 40-42). Specific articulations in the course of a public debate take these notions already in circulation and link them to particular policies, legitimating them and attributing them as actions to some particular actor. In this context, the question of whether 'situations of genocide' or 'severe human rights violations' justify 'humanitarian intervention' and promote 'the national interest' is considered extraneous. What matters is that these are the commonplaces invoked, and that the pairing of these commonplaces affords certain kinds of action while ruling others out. What makes this line of reasoning effective is precisely that it deploys existing commonplaces, so that the audience toward which the statement is directed will recognise the argument as sensible, and that it responds unequivocally to possible counter-arguments. Both of these components of a legitimation process are important aspects of this relational constructivist account (Jackson, 'Relational Constructivism: A War of Words').

9. The 'Somalia disaster' reveals how affect, empathy, and moral beliefs shape what is considered good, appropriate, and deserving of praise in situations where new norms emerge to compete with other norms and perceptions of interest. While initial support for intervention was strong, the brutal images of American soldiers being dragged through the streets in Mogadishu served to reinforce the boundaries between 'Americans' and 'foreigners' and the sense that the US government's primary responsibility as a moral actor is and should be the protection of American lives and interests.

10. The Clinton administration's response to Rwanda highlights the importance of separating individual and state morality. One of the dangers inherent in current approaches to addressing morality and moral responsibility in international relations is their tendency to collapse individual and state morality. Due to the moral complexity of state leadership, the moral stance of policy makers must be separated from the moral stance of individuals. Robert H. Jackson, *The Global Covenant: Human Conduct in a World of States* (Oxford: Oxford University Press, 2000) refers to the ethics of statecraft as 'a special ethical sphere'. Acting on the ideological reservoir of the state, policy-makers are at constant risk of losing moral authority by basing their decisions on precedence considerations in situations where their individual moral compass may not be compatible with state policy. This needs to be considered when analyzing the concept of moral responsibility in international relations.

11. Joao Marques de Almeida, 'Pluralists, Solidarists and the Issues of Diversity, Justice and Humantarianism in World Politics', *The International Journal of Human Rights* 7:2 (2003), 144-63.

9

The English School and Humanitarian Intervention

TIM DUNNE
UNIVERSITY OF QUEENSLAND, AUSTRALIA

Intervention for human protection is a key component of English School thinking about the rights and duties that states hold by virtue of their membership of international society. As a practice, it is as old as international society itself. A defence of intervention on humanitarian grounds can be found in the doctrine and practice of European great powers during the period when European hegemony was consolidated.[1]

Despite the persistence of the practice, humanitarian intervention has almost always been a divisive issue among diplomats, state leaders and world public opinion. It remains institutionally complex and normatively contested in world order today. The fissures in the international community were evident both during and after the NATO-led intervention in Libya in 2011. Supporters of the intervention were quick to argue that it was a 'textbook case',[2] while others argued that the intervention had risked doing irreparable damage to the responsibility to protect[3] 'norm' and its prospects for becoming the go-to framework for responding to atrocity crimes.[4]

Whether Russia and China were right to feel betrayed by the alleged shift in the Libya mandate from the protection of civilians to regime change, what is not in doubt is that the subsequent paralysis inside the Security Council has enabled the Assad regime to commit mass atrocities with virtual impunity. Despite the 'never again' slogan, Syria once again shows the limits of collective action on the part of international society to protect civilians experiencing unconscionable crimes.

The Libya intervention and the Syrian non-intervention show the complexity of the challenge that decision-makers encounter when considering how to respond to actual or potential mass atrocity crimes. One way to characterise the fissures and tensions in the debate is by utilising English School theorising on the intervention question. Not only are the language and concepts still relevant five decades after their elaboration, one could also argue that the category of pluralism is particularly relevant to how we think about state responsibilities in a post-Western world.

In an early contribution to post-Cold War debates about humanitarian intervention, Nicholas J. Wheeler argued that pluralism and solidarism constituted rival normative accounts of how the world hangs together.[5] Pluralists attach primary significance to the rules of coexistence that sovereign states have accepted as a means of maintaining order; they do so in the knowledge that there are widely diverse accounts of how to live 'the good life'. What might be considered just in one community could be considered depraved by another. For this reason, the starting point for a cooperative order is reciprocal recognition of sovereignty, an institutional arrangement where all peoples can build a community they call their own and the territorial borders of the sovereign state largely set the limits of that community. Sovereignty is therefore a defence of a way of life, and admission that 'states have the authority to make and enforce rules within a particular territory, therefore limiting the reach of foreign laws or external authorities'.[6] Intervention, even for human protection purposes, therefore violates a state's rights because it undermines a people's right to live without interference from outsiders.

Critics of pluralism charge that this sovereign state model has failed to deliver on its promise. The persistence of inter-state wars throughout the twentieth century suggests that sovereignty norms were not sufficient to deter predatory states. Moreover, the rule of non-intervention that was central to pluralism has enabled statist elites to violently abuse their own citizens with impunity.[7] The security of regimes has, in the pluralist order, taken priority over the security of peoples.

Recognising these concerns with the pluralist order, classical English School scholars such as Hedley Bull and R.J. Vincent were drawn to consider a different account of international society in which universal values such as the right not to be arbitrarily killed are more important than the principle of non-intervention. The guiding thought here, and one that is captured by the term solidarism, is that the ties that bind individuals to the great society of humankind are morally prior to the positivist rules and institutions that course through the veins of modern international society.

Bull originally defined solidarism as the collective enforcement of international rules and the guardianship of human rights.[8] Solidarism differs from cosmopolitanism in that the latter is agnostic as to the institutional arrangement for delivering universal values. While some cosmopolitans believe a world government is preferable, others following Kant think such a plan for world order risks unravelling into despotism. Solidarism is not a post-statist conception of international society; rather, it is one that is driven by states for the purposes and interests of the peoples they serve.

In a solidarist order, individuals are entitled to basic rights such as the right not to be indiscriminately killed or harmed. If harm is being undertaken on a large scale, and the sovereign state is either the perpetrator of the crime – or is unable to prevent it – then solidarists believe that the members of international society have a duty to intervene to protect peoples at risk.

Although Bull was drawn to the moral possibilities of a solidarist international society, he was also concerned that interventions, even for humanitarian purposes, risked undermining international order. Until there was a greater consensus on the meaning and priority to be accorded to rights claims, attempts to enforce them were premature and would likely do more harm than good. Writing in the mid-1990s, Wheeler and Dunne contrasted Bull's dilemma as one where his 'pluralism of the intellect' was pulling in a different direction to his 'solidarism of the will'.[9]

The solidarist case for humanitarian intervention gathered momentum through the 1990s, spurred on by the collective failure to prevent the genocide in Rwanda in 1994 and in Srebrenica in 1995. In both cases, the Security Council dithered, individual great powers looked the other way, and transnational civil society was mute when it ought to have been mobilising and shaming. For many inside the UN order, the problem for humanitarian intervention was not so much the danger that external powers were acting like cosmopolitan vigilantes showing no regard for the rules of the game; instead what was striking about the post-Cold War order was how little external powers were prepared to do in order to defend peoples against the worst crimes. 'Unhumanitarian non-intervention'[10] was much more apparent than great power 'sheriffs' and their middle power 'deputies' looking for opportunities to enforce the law. In truth, the pluralist rules of the post-1945 order had become far too enabling for governments to commit – or tolerate – egregious and systematic violations of the basic rights of their citizens. This was all too clear to then UN secretary general Kofi Annan – 'No government', he insisted, 'has the right to hide behind national sovereignty in order to violate the human rights or fundamental freedoms of its peoples.'[11]

Solidarist assumptions and commitments informed much of the thinking that took place on the intervention question inside the International Committee on Intervention and State Sovereignty (ICISS), the body funded by the Canadian government to review the conditions under which it is acceptable for coercive intervention to take place without host state consent. Much ink has been spilled on the Commission's findings, and how this epistemic community of global diplomats and scholars settled on the articulation of the responsibility to protect or R2P as it has become known.[12]

The change in the meaning of sovereignty from being an unconditional entitlement to being something that could be withdrawn if the state failed to meet certain civilised standards of behaviour signalled an important reform. But did the invention of R2P mark a shift from a pluralist conception of international society to a solidarist one that put the security of peoples ahead of the procedural concerns that protected the rights of sovereign governments? First and foremost, the reference for protection in the R2P framework is 'peoples' rather than states – suggesting a re-balancing of the largely state-based conception of rights and duties that are set out in the UN Charter. R2P starts with a presumption that prevention is better than cure; accordingly, all governments have to accept an obligation to protect their citizens from genocide, war crimes, ethnic cleansing and crimes against humanity. Yet R2P recognises that we live in an imperfect world where states frequently fail to uphold the moral and legal standards they have agreed to. In cases where a state is 'manifestly failing' to meet its responsibilities, the wider society of states is obliged to take a range of decisive measures to assist or coerce – with force being the instrument of the last resort.

In channelling all decisions involving the use of force solely through the Security Council, advocates of R2P underlined an ongoing preference for multilateralism and for working within the essentially pluralist institutions of the UN system – giving the five Permanent Members of the UN Security Council the power to block any action. Indeed, in a strong concession to pluralism, the great powers would only agree to paragraph 139 in the World Summit Outcome document – setting out the critical passage on the use of force – on the understanding that it merely codified existing responsibilities rather than created new ones.

At the same time, it is true that in implying that the international community had general and special responsibilities to act, R2P went well beyond the International Law Commission's findings on state responsibilities, which reduced international responsibility to nothing more than a bare pluralist injunction that states should cooperate with each other,[13] in the interests of the general good. One way to characterise the degree of moral ambition might be to say that there is more to responsibility in international relations than the pluralist suggests, but less than solidarists desire.[14]

The UN General Assembly resisted the view that intervention could take place without the consent of the Security Council if that body was unable to agree on a resolution when there was clear evidence of a humanitarian catastrophe happening – or about to happen. Yet the earlier ICISS report left open the possibility that other actors ought to act if the UN Security Council was deadlocked. The precise wording is worth further reflection: 'It is a real question in these circumstances where lies the most harm: in the damage to international order if the Security Council is bypassed or in the damage to that order if human beings are slaughtered while the Security Council stands by.'[15] What this ICISS statement and other recent work on moral agency force us to do is to consider a broad range of actors who 'each have a duty to contribute [...] and then to participate in an effective response',[16] rather than focus solely on the Security Council.

Despite the frequency of diplomatic statements supporting R2P, many fissures and fragments remain – some of which can be traced back to the co-mingling of universal meta-values of humanitarian protection with enforcement machinery that is heavily dependent on consensus. This co-mingling is evident when R2P is said to be a 'norm', a claim that is made frequently in both academic texts and practitioner speech-acts by global diplomats including the UN Secretary General. While it can be empirically shown that the phrase 'responsibility to protect' has increasingly found its way into UN Security Council resolutions, and countless diplomatic statements, we also know that its invocation can lead to radically divergent policy outcomes – timely action (as in the case of Libya) and relative indifference (as in the case of the 'forgotten war' in the Democratic Republic of Congo). Such inconsistencies are easily reconciled with a pluralist view of the world: the operation of the Security Council has always been on a 'case by case basis', meaning that military intervention is only ever going to be infrequent and subjected to coordination problems.

The fact that action in response to mass atrocities in one part of the world may have no bearing on a decision taken in response to violations elsewhere, leave R2P open to the charge of organised hypocrisy. It is often said, in this spirit, that there was no serious collective action in the early stages of the Syria crisis because of the 'betrayal' felt by Russia (and other countries) over the excessive force – and the expanded mandate – that characterised the NATO-led action against Libya. But one could argue that such a claim does not withstand much scrutiny: even without the so-called war of regime change against Gaddafi, inaction against Syria would most likely have been the outcome. Syria would have been Syria without Libya. For pluralists, inconsistency is a signal of competing priorities and complex risk assessments, such as when states reasonably judge that the costs of taking 'decisive action' to protect a target population may well be too great for their citizens to bear.

This challenge to articulate a conception of intervention that is more minimalist, and consistent with pluralism, had been taken up by Robert Pape.[17] His 'new standard' of 'pragmatic humanitarian intervention' is an attempt to ensure that R2P is aligned with a traditional pluralist conception of how key international institutions work – including the privilege of great powers on the UN Security Council who have the power to block action if they believe it to be contrary to their interests or detrimental to international order as a whole.

The conventional English School categories of pluralism and solidarism continue to capture the dynamics of intervention in international society. This does not mean that the English School is the only source of concepts to shed light on aspects of the intervention dilemma. Realism reminds us that coercive interventions seldom succeed and often exacerbate the problems that they were designed to resolve. Similarly, critical theorists point to the profoundly undemocratic character of deliberation within the R2P framework;[18] they also note that, in historical context, R2P looks very much like the 'executive' arm of the United Nations trying to impose a particular form of state-society relations on the global South following the collapse of formal empires in the early part of the twentieth century.[19]

Of the two conceptual categories suggested by Bull a half-century ago, it is solidarism that is looking vulnerable to the transformations that are under way. The narrative of a triumphant march of human rights and democratisation increasingly looks like an out-dated 'brand' now that the post-American era is upon us. If solidarism is fundamentally about the guardianship of human rights everywhere – including not only civil and political rights, but economic and cultural rights too – then perhaps its days are numbered. There is clearly no consensus about this wider basket of rights – and neither is there willingness to do the guardianship on the part of the powerful states in the world, nor the capacity on the part of international institutions.

Human protection, however, developed out of a coalition of states and civil society groups committed to ending the crime of genocide and other conscience shocking atrocities – it was never about upholding the entire basket of rights. And there is no doubt that there is a clear consensus among

UN member states that such atrocities are morally wrong as well as being deleterious to international peace and security. Agreement on condemnation has proven easier to forge than 'a common course of action even in the face of mass atrocities.'[20] Shorn of its complacency, a reinvigorated pluralist defence of responsibility is what is needed to bring greater reliance to R2P in our deeply divided world: after all, pluralism is on the side of states rather than being a source of their de-legitimation.

Notes

1. Hugo Grotius, *The Rights of War and Peace,* edited and with an introduction by Richard Tuck, from the edition by Jean Barbeyrac (Indianapolis: Liberty Fund, [1682] 2005).

2. See for instance Thomas G. Weiss, 'RtoP Alive and Well after Libya', *Ethics & International Affairs* 25:3 (2011).

3. The responsibility to protect, or R2P, is a particular variant of humanitarian intervention that emerged in the first decade of the twenty-first century. It is beyond the scope of this chapter to trace the evolution of R2P and the intricacies of its relationship to humanitarian intervention. For an authoritative account of R2P, see Alex J. Bellamy, *The Responsibility to Protect: A Defense* (Oxford; New York: Oxford University Press, 2015); Alex Bellamy and Tim Dunne, eds, *The Oxford Handbook on the Responsibility to Protect* (Oxford: Oxford University Press, 2016, in press).

4. David Rieff, 'R2P, R.I.P.', *The New York Times*, November 7, 2011.

5. Nicholas J. Wheeler, 'Pluralist or Solidarist Conceptions of International Society: Bull and Vincent on Humanitarian Intervention', *Millennium – Journal of International Studies* 21:3 (1992).

6. Jennifer M. Welsh quoted in Rosemary Foot, 'The State, Development, and Humanitarianism: China's Shaping of the Trajectory of the R2P', in *The Oxford Handbook on the Responsibility to Protect*, eds Bellamy and Dunne (Oxford: Oxford University Press, 2016, in press), 12.

7. Ken Booth, 'Human Wrongs and International Relations', *International Affairs* 71:1 (1995).

8. Hedley Bull, 'The Grotian Conception of International Society', in *Diplomatic Investigations: Essays in the Theory of International Politics*, eds H. Butterfield and M. Wight (London: Allen & Unwin, 1966).

9. Nicholas J. Wheeler and Tim Dunne, 'Hedley Bull's Pluralism of the Intellect and Solidarism of the Will', *International Affairs* 72:1 (1996).

10. Simon Chesterman, 'Humanitarian Intervention and Afghanistan', in *Humanitarian Intervention and International Relations*, ed. J. M. Welsh (Oxford: Oxford University Press, 2003); '"Leading from Behind": The Responsibility to Protect, the Obama Doctrine, and Humanitarian Intervention after Libya', *Ethics & International Affairs* 25:3 (2011).

11. Kofi Annan, 'Statement by the Secretary-General of the United Nations – 55th Session of the Commission on Human Rights', April 7, 1999.

12. Gareth J. Evans, *The Responsibility to Protect: Ending Mass Atrocity Crimes Once and for All* (Washington: Brookings Institution Press, 2008).

13. J. Crawford, *The International Law Commission's Articles on State Responsibility:*

Introduction, Text and Commentaries (Cambridge: Cambridge University Press, 2002).

14. This phrase is adapted from Linklater: Andrew Linklater, 'The English School', in *Theories of International Relations*, ed. Scott Burchill (New York: Palgrave Macmillan, 2013), 90.

15. In Stephen Hopgood, *Keepers of the Flame: Understanding Amnesty International* (Ithaca: Cornell University Press, 2006), 139.

16. Toni Erskine, 'Coalitions of the Willing and Responsibilities to Protect: Informal Associations, Enhanced Capacities, and Shared Moral Burdens', *Ethics & International Affairs* 28:1 (2014): 139.

17. Robert A. Pape, 'When Duty Calls: A Pragmatic Standard of Humanitarian Intervention', *International Security* 37:1 (2012).

18. Aidan Hehir, *The Responsibility to Protect: Rhetoric, Reality and the Future of Humanitarian Intervention* (Basingstoke, New York: Palgrave Macmillan, 2012).

19. Anne Orford, *International Authority and the Responsibility to Protect* (Cambridge; New York: Cambridge University Press, 2011).

20. Foot, in *The Oxford Handbook*, eds Bellamy and Dunne.

10

Shifting Gears:
From Global to Regional
The English School and the
Study of Sub-Global
International Societies

YANNIS A. STIVACHTIS
VIRGINIA TECH, USA

The English School (ES) of International Relations has been known for its globalist perspective as the scholars associated with it have long asserted that international society at the global level is the framework within which to discuss international order and reach conclusions as to how to ensure its durability.[1] This research agenda has been reinforced by the post-Cold War international relations focus on globalisation. The globalising world, it has been maintained, is one best approached through the universal lens of interstate society.

ES' preoccupation with global international society should be understood in two ways:[2] first, ES scholars have been concerned with the expansion of the historical European international society and its gradual transformation to the contemporary global international society;[3] and second, they have sought to examine how order and justice are maintained within the global international society.[4] The fixation of the classical ES with global international society and its disregard for societal developments at the regional level is reflected in Hedley Bull's view that 'purely regional' integration as largely irrelevant, indeed, inimical to 'global social integration'.[5]

Despite its globalist perspective, the traditional ES literature did focus on the study of historical regional international societies and investigated both their interaction and expansion tendencies.[6] For example, Martin Wight examined the Greek and Persian international societies and explored their interaction both in times of peace and war.[7] It is important to note that the work of the classical ES was to a significant degree influenced by Arnold Toynbee who investigated the genesis and disintegration of various civilisations[8] as well as their interaction in space and time.[9]

Although the ES' globalist perspective has its origins in the study of the establishment and expansion of a particular regional international society, namely the European society of states and its gradual transformation to the contemporary global international society, it needs to be acknowledged that for classical ES scholars the study of the European international society was not an object of attention in its own right but rather, it deemed to be important because the global international society was seen to be a consequence of the former's expansion.[10] This 'fixation on the global scale' meant that sub-global developments suffered both from conceptual underdevelopment and intellectual scepticism.[11]

The anti-regionalism of classical ES writings has been recognised by those working within the reconvened English School. Those scholars realised that emphasis on global international society is insufficient as there are interactions between global international society, which has been analysed for long time, and regional level(s), whose existence has largely been neglected by the English School. As a result, the reconvened ES has sought to reconfigure its research agenda and focus more on the study of various world regions. Opening the regional level of analysis might have serious implications for understanding institutions and norms like sovereignty, diplomacy, balance of power and others which exist and are performed at both global and regional level as, in many cases, regions form their own sub-global (regional) international societies which co-exist with global international society. Yet concepts derived from a global perspective have significant purchase at the regional level.[12] For example, Bull's distinction between an international system and an international society[13] and the social distinctions of *Gemeinshaft* and *Gesselshaft*[14] are particularly relevant.

The purpose of this chapter is to review the English School (ES) literature associated with the study of sub-global international societies.

There is general agreement among ES scholars that the global international society of today is a 'thin' one, in the sense that it is pluralistic and heterogeneous; and that within the bounds of that society, there are several 'more thickly developed' 'regional clusters' in which the solidarist elements of international society are developed to a greater degree.[15] According to Barry Buzan, because the logic of anarchy works more powerfully over shorter rather than longer distances and because states living in close proximity with one another may also share elements of common culture, *gemeinschaft* types of international societies may exist within the confines of a global international society.[16] These, moreover, are places where a modern standard of 'civilisation' is at its most developed.[17] Moreover, Buzan argues that the uneven development of international society means that some parts of the contemporary global system have more developed regional international societies than others.[18]

While earlier reassessments, contending with the effects of globalisation, focused on differences with regard to institutions and major actors of international society[19] more recently, I and my colleagues have taken a critical stance in relation to the current assessments of global international society by examining international society from the perspective of regions.[20] Our main purpose is to explore whether the development of international society at the regional level promotes or undermines the global international society. Confronting the puzzle presented by the increasing regionalisation of world politics and the impact that this process has had on international society, we have taken as our point of departure the fact that the re-scaling of world politics towards the regional dimension challenges to a certain extent the validity of the global international society framework. In so doing, we address questions like: what is global international society today? Does global order require the existence of a global international society? What does the uneven historical development of international society mean for global and regional orders? How global norms are understood at the regional level? Is there any interaction between regional international societies and, if yes, then what does this interaction tell us about global order?

Three pillars sustain the purpose and the rationale of their effort: first, the need to inquire about new regional normative dynamics within the ES (i.e. to shed light on how and why international norms and institutions assume different contours and meanings in different regional contexts when the level of analysis shifts from the global to the regional level); second, the need to take into account geographical, as well as institutional diversity within international society; and third, the need to think more thoroughly of how norms and rules travel from one level to another, both presently and in the past.

The question about the role of regions and the effects they have on global international society has become even more pertinent with the emergence (or re-emergence) of several regional powers.[21] It is now legitimate to speak of several regional international societies with their own structural and normative frameworks divergent from the global level. Since the main challenge for international society as a research project rests on capturing common interests, managing unequal power and mediating divergent values,[22] how to respond to the regional phenomenon in its normative and structural disclosure is the key question for international society scholars.

In the ES literature, the Western community of states serves as the most obvious candidate for a sub-global international society. However, it has been demonstrated that the West constitutes a set of overlapping regional international societies with different degrees of thinness/thickness.[23] Within this literature, 'Europe' occupies a central place not only because the region conforms to the basic defining condition of regional inter-state society, but also because the possibility exists (although it will be unevenly realised) for a broadly integrative and solidarist movement towards cooperation and convergence.[24]

Roger Morgan has argued that some of the concepts used by the traditional ES scholars can help to illuminate the current functioning of the European Union (EU) seen as a body of states subject to a wide range of rules, both formal and informal.[25] Hartmut Behr also suggests that the idea and study of international society can be applied empirically to the EU as well as Europe as a whole.[26] Thomas Diez and Richard Whitman have employed the ES concepts of 'international society', 'world society' and 'empire' to reconfigure the debate about the nature of EU governance and to compare the EU to other regional international systems.[27]

Starting from Buzan's premise that regional international organisations may reflect the existence of regional international societies, I, Mark Webber and our colleagues have sought to demonstrate that NATO, the EU, the Council of Europe (CoE) and the Organization for Security and Cooperation in Europe (OSCE) point to the institutionalisation of international society at the sub-global/European level.[28] Examining the EU, Thomas Diez, Ian Manners and Richard Whitman conduct a comparison between the EU as a regional international society and the global international society as analysed by Hedley Bull. They argue that the five core institutions of international order identified by Bull (balance of power, international law, diplomacy, war and great powers) have been modified or replaced. As a result, they identify the new institutions of the European order as the pooling of sovereignty, the *acquis communautaire*, multilevel multilateralism, pacific democracy, member state coalitions and multiperspectivity.[29]

In a more recent article, Bettina Ahrens and Thomas Diez argue that the EU forms a regional international society that has transcended the rules of Westphalian state-centred pluralism.[30] However, they point out that the analysis of the consequences of this transcendence for global international society has, so far, been limited. For the most part, such studies have focused on the EU as a normative power, and even within that literature, there is much more attention given to the question of whether the EU acts as a normative power rather than to the consequences of its actions. This is intriguing given that Ian Manners, who originally coined the term, thought of the EU's ability to fundamentally transform the pluralist international society as the ultimate litmus test of normative power. By focusing on the issues of human rights and regionalisation, Ahren and Diez explore this question further and demonstrate that the EU contributes to a solidarisation of international society. In this sense, European Regional International Society (ERIS) does not undermine, but instead promotes, a global international society based on European/western norms and values.

Focusing on the transatlantic alliance, Webber contends that during the Cold War, NATO was part of the 'thick' or solidarist end of European international society characterised by a convergence of values, and a sense of cooperative endeavour and common community. This core of 'liberal solidarism' stood alongside a 'thinner' pan-European international society, characterised by pluralist features of state co-existence, limited cooperation and the dominance of procedural mechanisms, such as the balance of power, diplomacy and international law, for managing international politics. According to Webber, NATO's post-Cold War development, and particularly its experience of enlargement, has modified this picture in some respects. Enlargement has provided the basis for an extension of the 'thick' core of European international society as new members have become enmeshed in the institutional, political and social practices associated with the Alliance. He concludes that in seeking to consolidate both the thicker (solidarist) and thinner (pluralist) ends of European international society spectrum NATO has managed to succeed fully in neither enterprise.[31]

I and Mike Habegger suggest that the CoE was and remains an essential component of ERIS and that the evolving structures and functions of organisation demonstrate an ongoing commitment to a homogeneous European regional international society.[32]

Examining the OSCE, Georgeta Pourchot argues that the organisation has developed most of the elements necessary for a sub-global international society. She notes that the OSCE displays elements of both 'solidarism' and 'pluralism' and contributes to a thin–thick continuum of international society in a manner that is functionally and structurally relevant.[33] Similar conclusions have been reached by Habegger and I in our own study of the organisation.[34] Pourchot also demonstrates that some of the institutions of international society identified by Bull, such as the balance of power, international law and diplomacy are at work within the framework of the organisation concerned.[35]

Another strand within the Europe-related ES literature focuses on the development of sub-European international societies. For example, Laust Schouenborg analyses the formation of a Scandinavian international society over a 200-year period and develops the concepts of 'primary institution' and 'binding forces' as an analytical framework.[36]

One of the main research themes developed by the classical ES was the study of relations between the historical European international society and the states located on its periphery, such as Russia and Turkey.[37] It is interesting, therefore, to see what kind of relations exist currently between the core of ERIS, on the one hand, and Russia and Turkey, on the other.

According to Richard Sakwa, although Russia has formally adopted Western democratic norms, their implementation is impeded by both practical and political forms of resistance to the universalism proclaimed by the West.[38] He argues that Russia does not reject the norms advanced by the main institutions of European international society, but it objects to what it sees as their instrumental application. Sawka points out that as a neo-revisionist power, Russia insists on respect for territorial and governmental sovereignty. Consequently, he concludes, Russia does not repudiate engagement with international society, but at present is ready only for a relatively 'thin' version.

Pami Aalto argues that the EU offers Russia access to regional level international society with a 'thicker' set of institutions than are available in its relations with the United States and the Asian countries.[39] The fact that Russia identifies itself with Europe has driven it to experiment with some of the solidarist institutions typifying EU-centred societies, most notable the market. Therefore, the ambivalence one may observe in the current relations between the core of ERIS and Russia is not very different from the ambivalence of the historical relations between the core of the European society of states and Russia.

Finally, Iver Neumann argues that Russia's rationality of government deviates from present-day hegemonic neo-liberal models by favouring direct state rule rather than indirect governance. As a result, he expects that the West will not recognise Russia as a full-fledged great power.[40] Here, it should be noted that Neumann does not argue that Russia is not a great power. Adopting the ES understanding of the role of great powers, he rather argues that Russia will not be accepted by Western powers as one of the custodians of international order.

It seems that Russia's treatment of Ukraine and the reaction of the US and the EU to Russia's involvement and policies undermine Aalto's assessment while strengthening Neumann's claim.

While Turkey is regarded as an integral part of ERIS, yet it is not included in its core organisation, namely the European Union. Bahar Rumelili suggests that the EU relations with Turkey continue to be situated at the intersection of Europe's particularist impulses and universalist ambitions and the construction of European and Turkish identities vis-à-vis each other is likely to remain an important arena of contestation.[41] Some work of mine has provided a comparison between the treatment of Turkey by the EU and the treatment that the Ottoman Empire received from members of the historical European international society and identifies many similarities between the two processes.[42]

Another strand of ES scholarship focuses on the study of international society in other world regions to find out what factors contribute to their strength or weakness. For example, relating the study of regional international societies to the study of regional security in various world regions, Barry Buzan and Ole Waever have demonstrated how the presence or absence of mature regional international societies condition (in)security at the regional level.[43]

Applying ideas about international and world society to the Middle East, Barry Buzan, Ana Gonzalez-Pelaez and their colleagues provide a comprehensive overview of the history of the region and how its own traditions have mixed with the political structures imposed by the expansion of Western international society. They argue that the Middle East forms a sub-global international society that can be distinguished from the broader international system. However, this society has not reached a maturity degree comparable to that of the European regional international society.[44] Moreover, their work reveals the powerful and ongoing tensions among the Western-defined political order, the post-colonial state system and the strong transnational cultural elements in the region. Yet, it shows both the problems and the opportunities of thinking about international and world society in a regional context and uses the insights from that to cast new light on what it means to talk about international society at the global level.

Ayla Göl's recent work also explores the contested nature of a regional interstate society in the Middle East and demonstrates why global and regional international societies mutually evolve.[45] Göl explores the dynamics of complex interplay between global and regional international societies in the context of the expansion of international society and 'revolt against the West'. Focusing on the state, nationalism, and a common culture and civilisational identity as the social structure of a regional international society, Göl concludes that global and regional international societies mutually evolve despite civilisational differences.

In the past quarter century, the importance of Asia in international relations has grown exponentially. The international society approach of the ES has been one among several theories that have been utilised for explaining Asia's evolving position in international relations both within Asia and with the rest of the world.[46]

Barry Buzan, Yongjin Zhang and their colleagues investigate whether or not significant and distinct international social structures exist in East Asia and what this can tell us about international society both regionally and globally.[47] They argue that the regional dispute over how its states and peoples should relate to the Western-dominated global international society makes the existence of East Asian international society essentially contested. While this regional–global social dynamic is present in many world regions, it is particularly strong in East Asia.

In response to the excessive universalism in the ES theorisation, Zhang has conducted a critical investigation of the development of international society in East Asia.[48] He looks at how primary institutions of the Westphalian society of states, such as sovereignty and imperialism, are imposed upon and resisted by East Asian states in remaking international relations in East Asia and in dismantling the traditional regional order. Zhang considers the way in which East Asian states creatively accept, interpret, engage in and practice certain primary institutions of Western-global international society, sovereignty and market in particular, on their own terms in the post-colonial context. Variations in interpretation and practice of these two primary institutions, he argues, amount to East Asian regional contestations to Western-global international society. Zhang also examines the peculiar features of great power management as a primary institution as it operates and is practiced in East Asia and reflects on how in terms of both power politics and political economy the regional and the global are mutually constitutive. In so doing, he offers a social structural view of contested existence of regional international society in East Asia, with an emphasis on understanding the contingent nature of the emergence of regional international society, its fluid existence, and the problematic nature of its social boundaries.

Wang Qiubin focuses on the Northeastern Asia regional international society and argues that this did not come into being until the end of the Cold War, when the states recognised mutually sovereign equality. Qiubin argues that compared to the EU, regional international society is not mature in Northeast Asia and the core principles of the Westphalian system, such as territoriality and sovereignty still dominate the region.[49]

Connecting the ES approach with the increasingly important region of Southeast Asia, Linda Quayle offers a comprehensive assessment of this region-theory linkage.[50] In a more recent article, Quayle utilises the ES' pluralist/solidarist spectrum to map and compare responses to the issue of migrant workers.[51] According to Quayle, this case suggests three things: first, the complexity of the relationship between global and regional societies is exacerbated by the starkly diverging pluralist and solidarist streams within the former; second, that the informal, consensus-orientated methods of the Association of Southeast Asian Nations, though often criticised, have proved useful at global level in moving dialogue forward in this contentious area; and third, that regional international societies provide highly salient arenas for dealing with this issue, but still struggle with inter-regional difference and trans-regional challenges.

Building upon theoretical contributions from the ES, John Anthony Pella Jr. analyses how West-Central Africa and West-Central Africans were integral to the ways in which Europe and Africa came together from the fifteenth century through to the twentieth.[52] His analysis demonstrates that that the expansion of international society was driven by individual interaction, and was shaped by both Africans and Europeans.

Elaine Tan addresses the development of international society in Africa by analysing the African Peer Review Mechanism (APRM).[53] Tan views APRM as a platform through which an African international society and global international society have interacted. She begins her analysis by pointing out that the presence of regional international societies implies the presence of differentiation in global international society, and the possibility of a breakdown in global consensus and the fragmentation of global international society. However, Tan argues that while divergences between African and global international societies on democracy and political governance result in tensions, the APRM can be seen as a way to mediate and reconcile these divergent positions. This has to be seen in the context of an unequal global international society, dominated by a number of core states with an increasingly solidarist governance agenda, as well as the attempts of a largely pluralist African international society to manages its demands. While the APRM might represent an uneasy and unstable compromise, this suggests that the relationship between regional and global international societies is significantly shaped by the ability and willingness of states to create possibilities for such compromises.

Working from the perspective of the ES, Federico Merke provides a historical account of the development of international relations in South America and argues that the presence of a number of shared values and institutions among regional states offers the foundations for a distinct regional international society.[54] Merke also examines the strategic positioning of Brazil in South America and how South America relates to Brazil's rising status both globally and regionally.[55] He argues that Brazil shares a number of values and institutions with its neighbours that contribute to the existence and function of a distinct regional international society in South America. He thus challenges the materialist stance held by realism which envisages that secondary powers either balance or bandwagon the dominant pole and affirms instead that South America's strategies towards Brazil are more complex and nuanced than a simple polarity standpoint suggests.

It appears that the post-Soviet space has attracted the attention of ES scholars interested in the study of sub-global international societies. For example, in my own work I explore the entry of Russia into what Boris Yeltsin called 'community of civilised states'.[56] To this end, I examine the changes that the Russian Government under President Yeltsin had to introduce in order to achieve the country's admission into post-Cold War international society. I argue that these changes included the democratisation of the Russian political system, the transformation of the Russian economic system into a free market economy, and the integration of Russian foreign policy into the broader society of states.

Katarzyna Kaczmarska's work focuses on Russia and its 'near abroad'.[57] She argues that following the end of the Cold War and throughout the 1990s Russia was seeking to re-join the global international society. Among other things, this meant that Russia was expected to adjust and accept norms and rules established and propagated by mostly Western liberal states but hailed as common for the family of states. However, with Vladimir Putin's ascendance to power and the country's economic recovery followed by Moscow's more assertive stance on global affairs, Russia has increasingly been seen as the supporter of a pluralist vision of international society characterised by limited co-operation, respect for sovereignty and non-intervention. Kaczmarska argues that these depictions ignored the fundamental differences in Russia's approach towards relations between states in the regional and global perspective. While on the global scale Russia cherishes norms of sovereignty and non-intervention, the regional realm has been subject to a variety of moves compromising the sovereignty of post-Soviet states. For example, in the Commonwealth of Independent States (CIS), Russia has been ready and willing to engage in undermining states' sovereignty in a number of ways, such as attempting to establish a sphere of influence, directly intervening in a civil strives, policing borders, waging wars on 'humanitarian' grounds and stimulating separatisms, as well as undertaking less explicit interventionist activities of regional integration, security provision and development assistance. She concludes that Russia's approach to its most immediate neighbours cannot be subsumed under pluralist or solidarist vision of interstate relations and this highlights the difficulty of approaching the Russian global-regional split using the conceptual apparatus of the English School.

Georgeta Pourchot and I examine the degree of integration in Central Asia and suggest that within the contemporary heterogeneous global international society there exist some more homogeneous regional/sub-global international societies, with Central Asia constituting one of them.[58] We argue that during the Cold War the global international society was divided into two sub-global international societies, one of them formed by the Soviet Union and its allies. With the end of the Cold War and the collapse of the Soviet Union, Russia sought to re-establish its regional primacy through the establishment of a set of international organisations ranging from the Commonwealth of Independent States (CIS) to the Shanghai Cooperation Organization (SCO).

By analysing historical and contemporary discourses about Russia's civilisational status, Filippo Costa Buranelli explores an alternative way for the diffusion of norms and institutions of international society different from those of European 'expansion' or 'inclusion', namely that of 'mediated expansion'. In so doing, he views Russia as 'a periphery in the centre' and as a 'less civilized civilizer' in European international society. He discusses the penetration of the Russian Empire in Central Asia in a socio-historical perspective and argues that in the process of the expansion, Russia's Asiatic past weakened its status as a European power and the value of its colonial enterprise.[59]

Arctic international relations are a complex of political, economic, development and militaristic dimensions. Throughout the Cold War, the Arctic was a region of symbolic military competition between the United States and Soviet Union. However, post-Cold War conditions in conjunction with climate change have transformed the Arctic into an important world region in the sense that states began to assert their claims of national sovereignty over areas previously considered inaccessible. This has had important implications for the Arctic regional order.[60]

Oran R. Young has been a key participant in debates among international relations scholars about the dynamics of rule-making and rule-following in international society. He weaves together theoretical issues relating to the formation of international regimes and substantive issues relating to the emergence of the Arctic as a distinct region in world affairs.[61] Young discusses the international linkages involved in the institutional arrangements in the international society and highlights various types of linkages that give rise to the concept of an institution including the idea of institutional nesting, overlapped regime and clustered institution.[62] He then examines the nature as well as the significance of the above-mentioned institutional linkages in the international society with particular focus on the Arctic region.

Following Young's pioneer work, Robert Murray, Anita Dey Nuttall and their colleagues demonstrate the multifaceted and essential nature of circumpolar politics.[63] Their work provides the theoretical tools necessary to approach the study of the Arctic and includes comprehensive studies of the policies of the eight Arctic states, a discussion about those non-Arctic states pursuing Arctic goals of their own, and the various international institutional bodies and frameworks that address Arctic issues.

The fact that *gemeinschaft* types of regional international societies may exist within the confines of a global *gessellschaft* type of international society raises the possibility that some of them may face the challenge of expanding into regions with their distinctive cultures. For example, it has been convincingly shown that the EU constitutes a regional homogeneous international society embedded in a heterogeneous European international system.[64] Through the process of enlargement, however, the regional homogeneous European international society (EU) expands outward, gradually transforming the heterogeneous European international system, in which it is embedded, into a more homogeneous regional European international society.[65]

But how do expanding *gemeinschaft* societies incorporate members, which do not share their culture? Because the standard of 'civilisation' has fallen into disrepute, other standards have risen to take its place. Of particular importance is the standard of 'democracy', which encompasses several other associated concepts such as respect for human rights, the rule of law, and liberal economic development. This, along with its portrayal as a timeless universal concept, provides democracy with an advantage in the expansion of regional international societies. As such, democratisation has become a stand-in for the civilising project.[66] Drawing on the example of the EU, I have argued that 'membership conditionality' serves a role similar to that of the historical standard of 'civilisation'.[67] I have demonstrated the similarity between the contents of the Copenhagen criteria, whose purpose is to regulate the EU enlargement (expansion) process, and the contents of the standard of 'civilisation', and argued that unless candidate states fulfil these criteria, they cannot be admitted into the EU.[68] Democracy promotion thus became a central dynamic of enlargement not only for the EU but also for other European international organisations, such as the CoE and NATO.[69] European regional international society has consequently become heavily reliant on forms of conditionality and monitoring.

The imposition of the European historical international society upon the rest of the world provided the classical ES with an opportunity to study the interaction between regional international societies. However, the interaction between contemporary regional international societies has only recently attracted the attention of ES scholars. For example, I have been interested in investigating the interaction between ERIS, on the one hand, and the post-Soviet and Middle East international societies on the other.[70]

Thomas Linsenmaier has put forward a conceptualisation of various types of relationships that unfold between regional international societies.[71] In this context, the traditional notion of 'expansion' is found wanting in capturing the full range of relationships and is complemented by forms of co-existence and confrontation. Understood as ideal types, the three concepts (expansion, co-existence, clash) serve as analytical tools for making sense of the varied nature of inter-regional encounters. This is illustrated with regard to the relationship between the European international society and its Eastern neighbours in the aftermath of the 2004 EU enlargement. A more nuanced reading of the inter-regional highlights a constellation quite different from 'expansion' where the European society does not push into empty space but reaches out into an alternative order, opening the possibility of a clash between the European and a consolidating post-Soviet regional international society.

Since the creation of the contemporary global international society has been the result of the European expansion and the superimposition of the European society of states upon other co-current regional international societies, I and my colleagues have sought to examine the perceptions that people and states in various parts of the world hold about Europe and the European Union in order to find out whether these perceptions have anything to do with the historical expansion of Europe.[72] Our work has revealed that some of these perceptions can be partly attributed to the historical expansion of Europe and partly to EU policies that resemble those of the past.

It has been argued that for regional international societies to exist in their own right, they should have institutions that differ from those of the global international society. However, recent ES literature has shown that although the same institutions may operate both at the global and sub-global levels they may be given different interpretations or being the subject of a different understanding at the regional level. This implies that it is still possible for sub-global international societies to exist.

Jorge Lasmar, Danny Zahreddine and Delber Andrade Gribel Lage have mapped the reach of key universal norms and rules of Human Rights Law in international society while also mapping, at the same time, specific regional interpretations and practices of such norms.[73] This mapping exercise contributes to the ES research agenda and its discussions of regions by trying to trace a clearer picture of the normative and institutional borders within international society and thus provide an additional tool to understand how regional norms and practice constitute, interact and redefine the global international society. According to the authors, by mapping the normative architecture of the primary institution of international law through its key Human Rights' universal norms and rules it is possible to undertake a geographic analysis of its diffusion and density throughout international society. Hence, it is also possible to visually assess the reach of norms we take for granted as being universal. On the other hand, they argue, the mapping of regional interpretations and practices of 'global' norms allows identifying if these regionalisms do construct coexistent regional clusters of different 'international' normative systems within the system-level institution governing international society.

In a similar fashion, Costa-Buranelli argues that while regional international societies can adopt more or less institutions than those at the global level, they may take some institutions present at the global level to mean something different.[74] He demonstrates that the development of regional international societies is favouring the polysemy of institutions, whereby different international societies adopt the same institutions with different meanings and specific normative contents. His conclusion seems to strengthen Adda Bozeman's observation that although non-European political communities had to formally adopt European norms and institutions during the expansion of European society of states in practice they still assigned different meanings to these norms and institutions.[75]

But if institutions exist at the global level and they are framed, interpreted and adopted differently in several regional international societies, what are the prospects for the existence of a global international society? Does it still make sense to speak of a global international society? And what methodological challenges does this polysemy pose to the English School? These very important questions have provided the fertile ground for further investigation by the new generation of ES scholars.

Notes

1. Hedley Bull, *The Anarchical Society* (London: Macmillan, 1977).
2. See Barry Buzan, *An Introduction to the English School of International Relations* (Oxford: Polity, 2014); Cornelia Navari and Daniel Green, eds, *Guide to the English School in International Studies* (Oxford: Wiley-Blackwell, 2014); Andrew Linklater and Hidemi Suganami, *The English School of International Relations: A Contemporary Reassessment* (Cambridge: Cambridge University Press, 2006); Alex Bellamy, ed., *International Society and Its Critics* (Oxford: Oxford University Press, 2005); and Tim Dunne, *Inventing International Society* (London: Macmillan 1998).
3. Hedley Bull and Adam Watson, eds, *The Expansion of International Society* (Oxford: Clarendon Press, 1984).
4. See Andrew Hurrell, *On Global Order* (Oxford: Oxford University Press, 2007); Ian Clark, *The Vulnerable in International Society* (Oxford: Oxford University Press, 2013); Ian Clark, *Hegemony in International Society* (Oxford: Oxford University Press, 2011); Ian Clark, *International Legitimacy and World Society* (Oxford: Oxford University Press, 2007); and Barry Buzan, *From International to World Society?* (Cambridge: Cambridge University Press, 2004).
5. Bull, *The Anarchical Society*, 281.
6. See Hebert Butterfield and Martin Wight, eds, *Diplomatic Investigations* (London: Allen & Unwin, 1966); and Adam Watson, *The Evolution of International Society* (London: Routledge, 1992).
7. Martin Wight, *Systems of States* (Leicester: Leicester University Press, 1977).
8. Arnold Toynbee, *A Study of History*, Abridgement of vols I-VI (Oxford: Oxford University Press, 1947).
9. Arnold Toynbee, *A Study of History*, Abridgement of vols VII-X (Oxford: Oxford University Press, 1957); and Arnold Toynbee, *The World and the West* (London: Oxford University Press, 1953).
10. Yannis A. Stivachtis and Mark Webber, 'Regional International Society in Post-Enlargement Europe', in *Europe After Enlargement*, eds Yannis A. Stivachtis and Mark Webber (London: Routledge, 2014), 9.
11. Barry Buzan, 'The Middle East through English School Theory', in *International Society and the Middle East: English School Theory at the Regional Level*, eds Barry Buzan and Ana Gonzalez-Pelaez (New York: Palgrave Macmillan, 2009), 28.
12. Stivachtis and Webber, 'Regional International Society in Post-Enlargement Europe', 10.
13. Bull, *The Anarchical Society*, 9-10, 14.
14. Barry Buzan, 'From International System to International Society: Structural Realism and Regime Theory Meet the English School', *International Organization* 47 (1993), 327–52.
15. See Yannis A. Stivachtis, 'The Regional Dimension of International Society', in *Guide to the English school in International Studies*, eds Navari and Green, 109-26; and 'International Society: Global/Regional Dimensions and Geographic Expansion', in *The International Studies Encyclopedia*, ed. Robert A. Denemark (Oxford: Wiley-

Blackwell, 2010), vol. VII, 4543-61.

16. Buzan, 'From International System to International Society', 333.

17. Yannis A. Stivachtis, 'Civilization and International Society: The Case of European Union Expansion', *Contemporary Politics*, 14:1 (2008), 71–90; and 'Civilizing' the Post-Soviet/Socialist Space: An English School Approach to State Socialization in Europe – The Cases of NATO and the Council of Europe', *Perspectives: Central European Review of International Relations* 18:2 (2010), 5-32.

18. Buzan, 'From International System to International Society', 344-5.

19. Richard Little and John Williams, eds, *The Anarchical Society in a Globalized World* (Basingstoke: Palgrave, 2006); and Yannis A. Stivachtis, ed., *International Order in a Globalizing World* (Aldershot: Ashgate, 2007).

20. Yannis A. Stivachtis, ed., *Interrogating Regional International Societies, Questioning the Global International Society*; special issue of *Global Discourse*, 5:3 (2015).

21. Barry Buzan and Ole Waever, *Regions and Powers* (Cambridge: Cambridge University Press, 2003).

22. See Hurrell, *On Global Order*.

23. Yannis A. Stivachtis, 'The Overlapping of Regional International Societies: The Case of the Transatlantic Community and the European Union', in *Global Politics in the Dawn of the 21st Century*, ed. Akis Kalaitzidis (Athens: ATINER, 2010), 389-409.

24. Mohammed Ayoob, 'From Regional System to Regional Society: Exploring Key Variables in the Construction of Regional Order', *Australian Journal of International Affairs* 53:3 (1999), 247-60, 248-9.

25. Roger Morgan, 'A European 'Society of States' – But Only States of Mind?' *International Affairs* 76:3 (1999), 559-74.

26. Hartmut Behr, 'Europe: History, Violence and "Peripheries"', *Review of European Studies* 4:3 (2011), 7-17; and Hartmut Behr, 'The European Union in the Legacies of Imperial Rule?' *European Journal of International Relations* 13:2 (2007), 239-62.

27. Thomas Diez and Richard Whitman, 'Analysing European Integration: Reflecting on the English School', *Journal of Common Market Studies*, 40 (2002), 43-67.

28. Stivachtis and Webber, eds, *Europe after Enlargement*.

29. Thomas Diez, Ian Manners and Richard Whitman, 'The Changing Nature of International Institutions in Europe: The Challenge of the European Union', in *Europe After Enlargement*, eds Stivachtis and Webber, 17-38.

30. Bettina Ahreans and Thomas Diez, 'Solidarization and its Limits: The EU and the Transformation of International Society', in *Interrogating Regional International Societies, Questioning the Global International Society,* ed. Yannis A.Stivachtis; special issue of *Global Discourse*, 5:3 (2015).

31. Mark Webber, 'NATO: Within and Between European International Society', in *Europe After Enlargement*, eds Stivachtis and Webber, 39-58.

32. Yannis A. Stivachtis and Mike Habegger, 'The Council of Europe: The Institutional Limits of Contemporary European International Society?' in *Europe After Enlargement*, eds Stivachtis and Webber, 59-78.

33. Georgeta Pourchot, 'The OSCE: A Pan-European Society in the Making?' in *Europe After Enlargement*, eds Stivachtis and Webber, 79-96.

34. Yannis A. Stivachtis and Mike Habegger, 'The OSCE as a Regional International Society', in *International Relations, Culture, and Global Finance*, ed. Akis Kalaitzidis (Athens: ATINER, 2011), 35-60.

35. Pourchot, 'The OSCE: A Pan-European Society in the Making?'

36. Laust Schouenborg, *The Scandinavian International Society: Primary Institutions and Binding Forces, 1815-2010* (Routledge: London, 2012).

37. See Adam Watson, 'Russia and the European States System', in *The Expansion of International Society*, eds Bull and Watson, 61-74; Thomas Naff, 'The Ottoman Empire and the European States System', in *The Expansion of International Society*, eds Bull and Watson, 143-70; Iver Neumann and Jennifer Welsh, 'The Other in European Self-Definition', *Review of International Studies* 17:4 (1991), 327-48; Iver Neumann, *The Uses of the 'Other': The 'East' in European Identity Formation* (Minneapolis: Minnesota University Press, 1998), ch. 2 and 3; Iver Neumann, *Russia and the Idea of Europe* (London: Routledge, 1996); and Iver Neumann, 'Entry into International Society Reconceptualized: The Case of Russia', *Review of International Studies* 37 (2011), 463-84.

38. Richard Sakwa, 'Russia and Europe: Whose Society?' in *Europe After Enlargement*, eds Stivachtis and Webber, 97-114.

39. Pami Aalto 'Russia's Quest for International Society and the Prospects for Regional-level International Societies', *International Relations* 21:4 (2007), 459-78.

40. Iver Neumann, 'Russia as a Great Power, 1815–2007', *Journal of International Relations and Development* 11 (2008), 128-51.

41. Bahar Rumelili, 'Turkey: Identity, Foreign Policy, and Socialization in a Post-Enlargement Europe', in *Europe After Enlargement*, eds Stivachtis and Webber, 35-49.

42. Yannis A. Stivachtis, 'Europe and the 'Turk': An English School Approach to the Study of EU–Turkish Relations', in *Turkey-European Union Relations: Dilemmas, Opportunities and Constraints*, eds Meltem Muftuler-Bac and Yannis A. Stivachtis (Lanham, MA: Rowman & Littlefield, 2008), 17-40.

43. Buzan and Waever, *Regions and Powers*.

44. Buzan and Gonzalez-Pelaez, eds, *International Society and the Middle East*.

45. Ayla Gol, 'Imagining the Middle East: The State, Nationalism and Regional International Society', in *Interrogating Regional International Societies, Questioning the Global International Society*, ed. Yannis A. Stivachtis; special issue of *Global Discourse* 5:3 (2015).

46. See Shaun Narine, 'The English School and ASEAN', in *Theorizing Southeast Asian Relations*, eds Amitav Acharya and Richard Stubbs (London: Routledge, 2008), 71-90; and Barry Buzan, 'The International Society Approach and Asia', in *The Oxford Handbook of the International Relations of Asia*, eds Saaadia Pekkanen, John Ravenhill and Rosemary Foot (Oxford: Oxford University Press, 2014), 100-19.

47. Barry Buzan and Yongjin Zhang, eds, *Contesting International Society in East Asia* (Cambridge: Cambridge University Press, 2014).

48. Yongjin Zhang, 'Regional International Society in East Asia? A Critical Investigation', in *Interrogating Regional International Societies, Questioning the Global International Society*, ed. Yannis A. Stivachtis; special issue of *Global Discourse* 5:3 (2015).

49. Wang Qiubin, 'On the Northeastern Asia Regional International Society', The Institute of International Studies, Jinlin University, China, 2007.

50. Linda Quayle, *Southeast Asia and the English School of International Relations* (New York: Palgrave Macmillan, 2013).

51. Linda Quayle, 'Leading or Following? International Societies, Southeast Asia, and the Issue of Migrant Workers', in *Interrogating Regional International Societies, Questioning the Global International Society*, ed. Yannis A. Stivachtis; special issue of *Global Discourse* 5:3 (2015).

52. John Anthony Pella Jr., *Africa and the Expansion of International Society* (London: Routledge, 2014).

53. Elaine Tan, 'The African Peer Review Mechanism (APRM): Interactions between African and Global International Societies', in *Interrogating Regional International Societies, Questioning the Global International Society*, ed. Yannis A. Stivachtis; special issue of *Global Discourse* 5:3 (2015).

54. Federico Merke, 'Unpacking South American International Society: A Historical Sketch', in *Regions in International Society: The English School at the Sub-Global Level*, ed. Ales Karmazin (Brno: Masaryk University 2014), 68-87.

55. Federico Merke, 'Neither Balance nor Bandwagon: South American International Society Meets Brazil's Rising Power', *International Politics* 52 (2015), 146-62.

56. Yannis A. Stivachtis, 'Liberal Democracy, Market Economy, and International Conduct as Standards of 'Civilization' in Contemporary International Society: The Case of Russia's Entry into the 'Community of Civilized States', *Journal of Eurasian Studies* 6 (2015), 130-42.

57. Katarzyna Kaczmarska, 'Russia's *droit de regard*: Pluralist Norms and the Sphere of Influence', in *Interrogating Regional International Societies, Questioning the Global International Society*, ed. Yannis A. Stivachtis; special issue of *Global Discourse* 5:3 (2015).

58. Georgeta Pourchot and Yannis A. Stivachtis, 'International Society and Regional Integration in Central Asia', *Journal of Eurasian Studies* 5:1 (2014), 68-76.

59. Filippo Costa Buranelli, 'Knockin' on Heaven's Door: Russia, Central Asia and the Mediated Expansion of International Society', *Millennium: Journal of International Studies* 42 (2014), 817-36.

60. Fugio Ohnishi, 'The Struggle for Arctic Regional Order', *Eurasia Border Review* 5:2 (2014), 81-97.

61. Oran Young, *Creating Regimes: Arctic Accords and International Governance* (Ithaca: Cornell University Press, 1998).

62. Oran Young, 'Institutional Linkages in International Society: Polar Perspectives', *Global Governance* 2:1 (1996), 1-23.

63. Robert W. Murray and Anita Dey Nuttall, eds, *International Relations and the Arctic* (Cambria Press, 2014).

64. Diez and Whitman, 'Analysing European Integration'.

65. Yannis A. Stivachtis, 'Understanding the European Union's Enlargement: The International Society Approach of the English School', in *The United States and Europe: Policy Imperatives in a Globalizing World*, ed. Howard Hensel, Global Interdisciplinary Studies Series (Aldershot: Ashgate, 2002), 55-77; Andrea Riemer and Yannis A. Stivachtis, 'European Union's Enlargement, the English School and the Expansion of Regional International Societies', in *Understanding European Union's Mediterranean Enlargement: The English School and the Expansion of Regional International Society*, eds Andrea Riemer and Yannis A. Stivachtis (Frankfurt: Peter Lang. 2002), 15-40.

66. Ian Clark, 'Democracy in International Society: Promotion or Exclusion?' *Millennium: Journal of International Studies* 37:3 (2009), 563-81.

67. Stivachtis, 'Civilization and International Society' and 'Civilizing' the Post- Soviet/ Socialist Space'.

68. Yannis A. Stivachtis and Brandon Kliewer, 'Democratizing and Socializing Candidate States: The Case of the EU Conditionality', in *The State of European Integration*, ed. Yannis A. Stivachtis (Aldershot: Ashgate, 2007), 143-60.

69. Stivachtis and Webber, *Europe after Enlargement.*

70. Yannis A. Stivachtis, 'European Union, Conditionality and Empire', in *Revisiting the European Union as Empire*, eds Hartmut Behr and Yannis A. Stivachtis (London: Routledge 2015), 74-96; 'Understanding the European Union's Enlargement;' and 'European Union's Enlargement, the English School and the Expansion of Regional International Societies'.

71. Thomas Linsenmaier, 'The Interplay between Regional International Societies', in *Interrogating Regional International Societies, Questioning the Global International Society*, ed. Yannis A. Stivachtis; special issue of *Global Discourse* 5:3 (2015).

72. Yannis A, Stivachtis, ed., *Europe and the* World, special issue of the *Review of European* Studies 4:3 (2012).

73. Jorge Lasmar, Danny Zahreddine and Delber Andrade Gribel Lage, 'Understanding Regional and Global Diffusion in International Law: The Case for a Non-Monolithic Approach to Institutions', in *Interrogating Regional International Societies, Questioning the Global International Society*, ed. Yannis A. Stivachtis; special issue of *Global Discourse* 5:3 (2015).

74. Filippo Costa Buranelli, 'Do you know what I mean?' 'Not exactly': English School, Global International Society and the Polysemy of Institutions', in *Interrogating Regional International Societies, Questioning the Global International Society*, ed. Yannis A. Stivachtis; special issue of *Global Discourse* 5:3 (2015); and 'Regional International Societies, the Polysemy of Institutions and Global International Society', E-International Relations, 1 August, 2013.

75. Adda Bozeman, *Politics and Culture in International History* (Princeton: Princeton University Press, 1960), 5-6; and Adda Bozeman, *The Future of Law in a Multicultural World* (Princeton: Princeton University Press, 1971), ix.

11

Another Revolt Against the West?

JASON RALPH
UNIVERSITY OF LEEDS, UK

In his contribution to Part III of the English School 1985 classic *The Expansion of International Society*, Hedley Bull describes what he called 'the revolt against the West'.[1] At the turn of the twentieth century, Bull argued, European and Western powers 'expressed a sense of self-assurance, both about the durability of their position in international society and its moral purpose.'[2] That, however, did not survive the First World War. From that point on a revolt against western dominance unfolded in 'five phases or themes', which Bull identified as an anti-colonial revolution and the struggle for equal sovereignty, racial equality, economic justice and cultural liberation. This was brought about by five factors. There was, Bull argued, a 'psychological awakening' in the non-Western world, 'a weakening of the will on the part of the Western powers to maintain their position of dominance, or to at least accept the costs necessary to do so', the rise of new powers such as the Soviet Union, 'a more general equilibrium of power' and 'a transformation of the legal and moral climate of international relations' which was influenced by the majorities of votes held by Third World states.

It is tempting to read this narrative into an analysis of contemporary international society. The coordination of positions by the BRICS – Brazil, Russia, India, China and South Africa – represents some kind of psychological awakening; a post-Iraq, post-Great Recession United States suggests a weakening of the West's willingness to maintain its position of dominance; and the rise of China promises the return of a general balance of power. These parallels need to be qualified. Christopher Layne's argument that this time predictions of American decline are real is for instance contested, and so is the idea that BRICS is anything more than an acronym that conveniently frames the photo opportunities of non-Western leaders.[3]

There is, however, something in Bull's analysis that offers an interesting angle on contemporary international society. Bull noted in 1985 for instance how the grouping together of Third World states had transformed their subject status and helped to change the legal and moral climate across international society.

The equal rights of non-Western states to sovereignty, the rights of non-Western peoples to self-determination, the rights of non-white races to equal treatment, non-Western peoples to economic justice, and non-Western cultures to dignity and autonomy – these are today clearly spelt out in conventions having the force of law.[4]

Central to this was the ability of these states 'to call upon the prestige of numbers, not merely of states but of persons, accruing to the states claiming to represent a majority of the world's population'.[5] Implicit in this formulation is the argument that the norms and laws that characterise international society are responsive to legitimacy claims that are based on a democratic ethos of representativeness.

This is relevant today because it draws attention to the exclusionary hierarchies contained in contemporary international society and how they cannot be legitimised by 'the prestige of numbers'. The exclusion of India – the world's largest democracy – from permanent UN Security Council status is testament to that. It also sheds light on that aspect of the BRICS agenda which seeks to hold western governments to account before the international mandates of institutions like the UN Security Council and to reform those institutions so that they are more representative. Their reaction to the Libyan intervention and the Brazilian call for a 'Responsibility while Protecting' can be partially understood in this context.

When English School scholarship highlights 'the prestige of numbers' and the normative power of representativeness, it does not necessarily mean it is a voice advocating reform. Its understanding of international society has always placed democratic values like representativeness and accountability in a normative framework where international order, and the power to guarantee it, is also valued. In this sense the exclusionary hierarchies of the UN Security Council as well as less representative forms of hegemony like American empire might be valued if they effectively provide public goods like order. This is especially so if they can encourage 'followership'. Recent English School scholarship captures this debate extremely well. Andrew Hurrell, for instance, juxtaposes 'effectiveness' alongside 'representation', noting that:

> Those who reject calls for a reform and expansion of the permanent membership of the Security Council often rest their

arguments on the importance of effectiveness. Yes, reform might promote representation, but at what cost? If a Council of 25 or 26 is even less able to act effectively than the current arrangement, then how has this increased the legitimacy of the organization?[6]

Ian Clark, too, notes how the Security Council often requires American support to be effective, which invariably requires granting the US the kind of latitude that risks delegitimising the Council in the eyes of other states. He adds that expanding the Council on 'symbolic' rather than 'material' grounds runs the risk of widening the gulf between its representative legitimacy, and its efficacy-based legitimacy, all the more so if any expansion of permanent membership were in some way explicitly intended to constrain the influence of the United States.[7]

An 'efficacy-based' conception of legitimacy may, in other words, confer 'special rights and responsibilities on the state with the resources to lead' in ways that counteract 'the prestige of numbers'.[8] This is the kind of 'middle way' thinking that characterises much of the English School thinking. For the BRICS, they may be able to combine efficacy-based arguments with a plea to representativeness in order to promote their voice in international decision-making. But for others, any argument that prioritises efficacy over representation is bound to be seen as proof of the English School's conservative image.

Notes

1. Hedley Bull, 'The Revolt against the West', *The Expansion of International Society* (New York: Oxford University Press, 1985), 217-28.
2. Ibid., 219.
3. Christopher Layne, 'This Time it's Real: The End of Unipolarity and the *Pax Americana*', *International Studies Quarterly* 56:1 (2012), 203-13. See also debate between Layne, William Wohlforth and Stephen G. Brooks in Michael Cox and Doug Stokes, eds, *US Foreign Policy* (Oxford: Oxford University Press, 2012), 409-30.
4. Bull, 'The Revolt', 227.
5. Ibid.
6. Andrew Hurrell, *On Global Order: Power, Values and the Constitution of International Society* (Oxford: Oxford University Press, 2007), 87.
7. Ian Clark, *Hegemony in International Society* (Oxford: Oxford University Press, 2011), 153-4. See also Ian Clark and Christian Reus-Smit, 'Liberal Internationalism: The Practice of Special Responsibilities and Evolving Politics of the Security Council', *International Politics* 50:1 (2013), 38-56.
8. Ibid., 175.

12

From Cinderella to Beauty and the Beast: (De)Humanising World Society

MATTHEW S. WEINERT
UNIVERSITY OF DELAWARE, USA

For Barry Buzan to describe world society as the Cinderella concept of the English School was to announce that the time for glass slipper fittings has drawn nigh.[1] Imprecision regarding the concept and uncertainty as to what value it brought to our understanding and explanation of international relations owed to at least two sources. First, English School theorists tended to equate world society, ambiguously as it were, with humanity as a whole (a residue of earlier philosophical imaginations),[2] and, later, human rights and cosmopolitanism which tended, unintentionally or not, to blur if not conflate world society with solidarist international society.[3] Second, scholars from diverse theoretical orientations have further confused matters by attaching the label 'world society' to civilisations, communications systems, (international) crime, democracy, the economy, education, empire, the environment, global civil society, global governance, health, institutions, integration, law, migration, non-governmental organisations, regionalism, religion, security communities, technology, and transnational social movements.[4] More theoretically inclined works assay world society in the international relations terms of system, structure, and process, or the sociological ones of society and community. The sheer diversity of subjects linked to it suggests that world society has become something of a trope to capture a web of relations between diverse actors distinct from and operating outside the formal rubric of state governance reflective of (presumably) a commonality of interests, values, and normative commitments. On that reading, the systems or transactional view of world society, defined in terms of communication networks and the interaction capacity of systems,[5] is wed to the social view, defined in the (cosmopolitan) normative terms of shared values, rules and institutions.[6] Treated as a conceptual midden, it is no surprise that the very notion of world society eludes.

But Cinderella, so the fairy tale goes, rises from obscurity. Various trans-border processes, environmentalism, globalisation, and humanitarian sentiments no doubt have piqued interest in world society – even in ways that suggest world society, equable with global civil society, may also contain uncivil elements. This chapter aims to inject some energy into the concept, but does not do so by challenging the very notion that perhaps confuses world society: its equability with humanity writ large. Rather, in this limited space, I engage the world society as humanity notion in a way that might help extricate world society from the clutches of the international society of states so as to do for world society what has been done for international society: to develop an account of its primary institutions and pave a way forward for world society scholarship.

Certainly world society never attracted as much attention as its sister concept, international society, which has served in the classical English School tradition as the *via media* between realism/international system and revolutionism/world society. Broadly construed, world society 'implies something that reaches well beyond the state towards more cosmopolitan images of how humankind is, or should be, organized.'[7] Implication, though, is not certitude, and thus Buzan could aptly describe some views of world society as incredulous: it 'doesn't exist in any substantive form, and therefore its moral priority is unattached to any practical capability to deliver much world order'.[8]

Martin Wight anticipated that misgiving; none of the three methods he outlined for constructing world society have come to fruition.[9] Structural uniformity (e.g. Kant's plan for perpetual peace as a federation of states with republican constitutions) might inflame the expectations of modern-day democrats, and one might plausibly argue that successive waves of democracy have extended a realm of peace, but the inherent state-centrism of the perspective deflects attention away from *world* society and towards *international* society. Doctrinal or ideological imperialism (e.g. messianic universalism, whether secular – Napoleonic empire, Nazism, communism – or theological – al Qaeda's call for a resurrected caliphate) may attract followers, but such movements historically have been met with overwhelming force. Finally, cosmopolitanism, which prioritises the individual above (and perhaps against the state), may have the most traction for a contemporary audience predisposed to championing human rights and associated international public policies and institutions framed around improving human welfare, and thus offers promise for deep development in ways that 'assimilate international to domestic politics'.[10] Yet on this reading world society appears as code for domestic policy homogenisation, which occludes world society's distinctiveness.[11]

The need for (analytical and ontological) clarity may have compelled Bull to equate world society with 'all parts of the human community',[12] which James Mayall echoes with the 'view that humanity is one'.[13] But what this means in practice is questionable. It captures the aggregate of inter-human discourse and exchange. But contractual arrangements as exponentially increasing features of an increasingly globalised, commodified world constitute relations of exchange, yet do not lend any lasting depth to world society since contracts by definition terminate once their terms have been fulfilled. Mayall, taking a cue from Bull who defined world society in terms of commonality of interests and values that bind humanity as a whole, may help:[14] 'the task of diplomacy is to translate this latent or immanent solidarity of interests and values into reality'.[15] Non-English School scholarship – e.g. Theodor Meron's work on the humanisation of the laws of war, Ruti Teitel's *Humanity's Law*, and Erin Daly's study of dignity and comparative constitutional law – illustrate the extent to which Mayall's point has been realised in theory and practice.[16] However, while Mayall's approach tasks the researcher with identifying such interests and values, producing an account of how and why they arise, and assessing how they link otherwise disparate human beings together in ways that constitute and shape world politics, it replicates Wight's assimilationist, and in the end state-centric, view. World society disappears into the recesses of interstate social relations.

At this point, Buzan, seeing Cinderella donned in the most pedestrian of garb, completely re-outfits her: if her humanity-style failed to dazzle, perhaps a make-over focused on structural regularities, e.g. the world economy and even sub-global/regional projects that shape identities, interests, and roles, would prove to be the dressing gown that would transform her into a (not the) belle of the ball.[17] Leaving aside the thematic focus (e.g. the economy, sub-regionalism, environmentalism, etc.) suggested by his approach, this attention shift offers two important lessons for world society scholarship. First, it disposes of normative homogeneity implied by world society (e.g. its presumed solidarism). Actors come to have disparate interests and normative commitments based on their (uneven) roles in the world economy. Great variation in depth of commitment to regional integration projects likewise signify varying degrees of fragmentation. Second, the approach acknowledges there are multiple value and interest commitments held by individuals and the collectives into which they have allocated themselves (e.g., pluralism).[18] As earlier intuited by Wight and Gong, world society may not be that civil after all; Cinderella could actually be a dominatrix in disguise.

Put differently, if we subject the broad vision of world society as human community to an organisational schematic that does not hinge on a singular, cohesive logic but that admits multiplicity, then we expose the potentialities of, and the fractures impeding, world society's conceptual and practical development.

We might, then, tackle world society from a more primordial standpoint: how interhuman dialogue and social practices (re)constitute membership in the human community in both beautiful and bestial ways.[19] Gong and Wight previously engaged the notion that membership in humanity was contingent on understandings of civility and legitimacy, and thus illustrated that fragmented visions of world society cohabit the same analytical space as unitary notions of humankind.[20] As ethically appealing as the (cosmopolitan, biological) thesis that all *Homo sapiens* are human may be, we must acknowledge that distinct conceptualisations of what it means to be human have been the source of a whole lot of world (dis)order, especially if we think that imperial and apartheid systems were built upon the depravity of racially constructed notions of civilisation. From various '-isms' (e.g. racism, sexism, nationalism) and sundry other psychologically and socially embedded frames of reference have precipitated a range of dehumanising, exclusionary and oppressive practices – many laundered through the states-system which has magnified the effects of sometimes hierarchical, nearly always discriminating notions of world society qua humanity framed from particular, exclusive collectivist vantage points.

World society scholarship must invariably set and measure its cosmopolitan underpinnings against a history of dehumanisation. It makes little sense to replicate the dreams of the humanists given that Bosnians, Croats, Serbs, Hutus, Tutsis, capitalists, communists, rich, poor, middle class, whites, blacks, gays, straights, men, women, Muslims, Christians, Jews, Buddhists, Hindus, Arabs and countless 'types' of human beings have harboured, *and harbour*, animosity towards others (always under the guise of some iconoclastic justification). In some cases, groups have denied recognition of others *as (fully) human* and acted violently against those who they detest, or erected legal and political strictures to ensure their marginalisation or exclusion from socio-political relations and the protection of the law. Hate, disregard, and disparagement as social practices are too prevalent in human life, and have informed perverse organisational logics; we must, therefore, construct even our most aspirational of theories on dystopic facts.[21]

Kimberly Hutchings outlined the problem I underline here. The human being is 'fundamentally defined by the gap between "essence" and "existence"'. That is, unlike a table or a tree, 'the being of any particular human does not coincide with any given list of attributes'.[22] I recast the matter as a distinction between human *being* and being *human*. By the former I refer to a set of intersubjective understandings and standards, always specific to any given context, that determine who is recognised as fully human. These, in turn, are both informed by and limit being *human*, or the panoply of activities, projects, commitments, identities and memberships that give our particular lives meaning. Stated differently, being human refers to the various modes of becoming individual selves in ways that accord with the social yardstick of the human being. On this reading, dehumanisation stems from incongruity between one's particular mode of being human – say, a Jew in Nazi Germany, a woman in an androcentric society, or homosexual in a homophobic one – and prevailing conceptions of human being.

To capture this socially constructed phenomenon, I proposed a notion of making human centred on five processes that operate within and through (international) institutional sites: reflection on the moral worth of others, recognition of the other as an autonomous being, resistance against forms of oppression, replication (of prevailing mores), and responsibility for self and others.[23] Much of the work of making human occurs at the micro level of the individual, underscoring it as an interhuman, and thus world society, practice: e.g. encountering the other, bracketing attitudes and prejudices for the purposes of social cooperation if not harmony, learning that difference is not something necessarily to be feared or stigmatised, or coming to appreciate our neighbour not as an Other but as a decent human being. On this view, empathy and the hard work of introspection deliver us from solipsistic fear and disgust of difference. Yet we do not (or cannot) always disentangle ourselves from socially and doctrinally sanctioned prejudices that become an inherent part of our psycho-social makeup. Likewise, collectives cannot always force ideologues, racists, sexists, xenophobes and zealots to accept the other; the problem of making human thus extends beyond individual, psychological confines and presents itself as a macro phenomenon suitable for inquiry in world society scholarship.

Examination of these processes does not take human standing in society for granted. Rather, it poses new kinds of questions germane to understand how humanity (re)constitutes itself: how do various forms of inter-human interaction inform collective social structures and generate distinctive systems to organise the mass of human beings? In what ways does the categorisation of human beings help us better explain and understand the world society concept? In what ways do institutions of international society respond to more elemental forms of inter-human interaction that discern and then allocate 'types' of human beings into different organisational schematics with varying degrees of autonomy? Beauty, it seems, is right at home with the beast. The point of the world society concept, then, is to explore those many homes.

Clearly, I am concerned with developing the world society concept. In particular, might we tease out a set of primary (and by implication, secondary) institutions distinctly world society in orientation and hence do for it what has been done for international society?

I construe making human as a primary institution of world society, meaning 'durable and recognised patterns of shared practices rooted in values commonly held' that in the end 'play a constitutive role in relation to both the pieces / players and the rules of the game'.[24] Though discrete, the five humanising processes that constitute what I call in the aggregate making human exhibit what Wittgenstein called 'family resemblances'. Even if they may 'have no one thing in common', they 'are all related to one another in many different ways',[25] much like the 'resemblances between members of a family: build, features, colour of eyes, gait, temperament, etc. etc. [that] overlap and criss-cross'.[26]

Yet at least one question remains: what is the logical connection between humanising and dehumanising practices? How can both the beautiful and the bestial form world society? As practices designed to govern and manage human diversity and hence the very notion of human being, both humanisation (making human) and dehumanisation aim to construct world society in particular images: one ostensibly from a universal, inclusive standpoint, the other from a selective, exclusive standpoint. Interpreted dispassionately, both hint at a neglected insight into world society found in Hedley Bull's 1983 Hagey lectures. Writing about ecological matters, Bull observed that measures undertaken with respect to the dangers of disequilibrium between population and resources and other ecologically orientated issues 'take us beyond the sense of solidarity or common interests among governments' and into recognition of a common human interest 'in maintaining itself'.[27]

The awful truth is that human beings – the irreducible elements of world society – may seek to maintain themselves and the broader society they presumably form by acknowledging and accepting the diversity of ways of being human, or by protecting and conserving specifically defined communities of people against the presumed malignancy posed by hated others. In the end, world society as humanity is both beauty and beast; the concept thus ought to capture the complexity of ways human beings manage the very plurality of the human condition and grapple with the paradox that while we can belong anywhere, nowhere has proven more vexing than belonging to humanity itself.

Notes

1. Barry Buzan, *From International to World Society? English School Theory and the Structure of Globalisation* [*FIWS?*] (Cambridge: Cambridge University Press, 2004), 11. Buzan reframes the traditional triad of international system, international society and world society as interstate societies (asocial, Hobbesian, Pluralist, Solidarist, Kantian and [con]federative types), transnational societies (pure medievalism, transnational coalitions across type and among similar transnational associations, competing transnational associations and no transnational associations), and interhuman societies (constituted by universal identities, large-scale imagined communities or fragmented ones in the form of families/clans) at 133.

2. E.g. 'The world society, the social cosmos – there could be other terms for it – is sometimes, in particular, referred to as the multi-state system (the system, that is, of many sovereign states). But the subject to be studied is not just the system of states. It is human society, comprehensively, as a whole.' He continues in a manner that anticipates Buzan's reconstruction of the English School conceptual triad:
'call it the many-levelled society, with the multistate system as the layer at the top, not altogether unlike the water-lily-covered surfaces of a series, or system, of ponds (the lilies drawing nourishment from mostly invisible sources down below). Two below-the-surface levels, at least, require separate recognition. Basic to the whole is the level of human life as physically, biologically, and psychologically lived—the life of men and women and of men-and-women-to-be. And intermediate between the actual life of human units, and the notional life of states, there is the complicated habitat in which there live and have their hybrid part-actual-part-notional being the numberless and variegated assortment of groups, groupings and organisations, in and through which men associate together to strive the more effectively for ends they have in common.' C.A.W. Manning, *The Nature of International Society* (New York: Wiley & Sons, 1975), 34.

3. E.g. R.J. Vincent, *Human Rights and International Relations: Issues and Responses* (Cambridge: Cambridge University Press, 1986); and R.J. Vincent, 'Grotius, Human Rights, and Intervention', in *Hugo Grotius and International Relations*, eds Hedley Bull, Benedict Kingsbury and Adam Roberts (Oxford: Clarendon Press, 1990).

4. This accounting is based on a simple search of the term 'world society' in the academic database JSTOR.

5. Niklas Luhmann, 'World Society as a Social System', *International Journal of General Systems* 8:3 (1982), 131-38.

6. See Vincent, *Human Rights and International Relations*.

7. Buzan, *FIWS?*, 1.

8. Ibid., 36.

9. Martin Wight, *International Theory: The Three Traditions*, eds Gabriele Wight and Brian Porter (New York: Holmes & Meier, 1992), 40-48.

10. Ibid., 46.

11. R.J. Vincent quoted in Buzan, *FIWS?*, 51: 'a fully solidarist international society would be virtually a world society because all units would be alike in their domestic laws and values on humanitarian intervention'. See also Fred Halliday, 'International Society as Homogeneity: Burke, Marx, Fukuyama', *Millennium* 21:3 (1992), 435-61.

12. Hedley Bull, *The Anarchical Society: A Study of Order in World Politics* (New York: Columbia University Press, 1995), 269. See also Barry Buzan, 'From International

System to International Society: Structural Realism and Regime Theory Meet the English School', *International Organization* 47:3 (1993), 337.

13. James Mayall, *World Politics: Progress and its Limits* (Cambridge: Polity Press, 2000), 14.

14. Bull, *The Anarchical Society*, 269.

15. Mayall, *World Politics*, 14.

16. Theodor Meron, 'The Humanization of Humanitarian Law', *The American Journal of International Law* 92:2 (2000), 239-78; Theodor Meron, 'The Martens Clause, Principles of Humanity, and Dictates of Public Conscience', *The American Journal of International Law* 94:1 (2000), 78-89; Ruti Teitel, *Humanity's Law* (New York: Oxford University Press, 2011); and Erin Daly, *Dignity Rights: Courts, Constitutions, and the Worth of the Human Person* (Philadelphia: University of Pennsylvania Press, 2013).

17. Barry Buzan, International Political Economy and Globalization', in *International Society and its Critics*, ed. Alex J. Bellamy (New York: Oxford University Press, 2005), 115-33. In the same volume, Matthew Patterson considers the environment. 'Global Environmental Governance', 163-78.

18. See John Williams, 'Pluralism, Solidarism, and the Emergence of World Society in English School Theory', *International Relations* 19:1 (2005), 19-38.

19. On the concept of practice, see Cornelia Navari, 'The Concept of Practice in the English School', *European Journal of International Relations* 147:4 (2010), 611-30.

20. See Martin Wight's chapter on 'Theory of Mankind: 'Barbarians'' in *International Theory*, 49-98, and Gerritt Gong, *The Standard of 'Civilization' in International Society* (Oxford: Clarendon Press, 1984).

21. On this point I write in the spirit of Judith Shklar, 'Putting Cruelty First', *Daedalus* 111:13 (1982), 17-27.

22. Kimberly Hutchings, 'Simone de Beauvoir', in *Critical Theorists and International Relations, eds* Jenny Edkins and Nick Vaughan-Williams (Abingdon and New York: Routledge, 2009), 67.

23. *Making Human: World Order and the Global Governance of Human Dignity* (Ann Arbor: University of Michigan Press, 2015).

24. Buzan, *FIWS?*, 181.

25. Ludwig Wittgenstein, *Philosophical Investigations*, trans. G.E.M. Anscombe (New York: MacMillan, 1958), 31.

26. Ibid., 32.

27. Hedley Bull, *Justice in International Relations* (Waterloo, CA: University of Waterloo, 1983), 14.

13

Pluralism and International Society

TOM KEATING

UNIVERSITY OF ALBERTA, CANADA

Much attention among English School scholars is devoted to developing the concept of international society through an exploration of its relationship with its alternatives: international system and world society.[1] One of the distinguishing characteristics of international society is its attention to a plurality of states operating within a mutually recognised society. The idea of pluralism and a pluralism based on autonomous states has thus been central to thinking about international society. Yet the idea and practice of pluralism has been questioned by a number of observations. One is a view that pluralism does not accurately account for an international society deeply embedded within Eurocentric practices and ruled by Western values that have been imposed on non-Western states through imperial practices.[2] A second concern has been raised by Andrew Hurrell, who questions pluralism on the grounds that is unable to meet the pressing needs of the global community from environmental threats to the complex web of global finance to demands emanating from economic inequalities and identity politics. 'The changes associated with globalisation and the increased interaction and connectedness across global society have therefore undermined both the practical viability and the moral acceptability of a traditional state-based pluralism.'[3] Practices of economic globalisation and human security have generated a third set of observations about the extent of more intrusive forms of global governance – that now regulate or supersede the authority of sovereign states and diminish the extent and significance of state-based pluralism within international society. Matthew Weinert recounts that:

> States increasingly face robust homogenizing pressures in the form of (a) transparent and accountable governance yardsticks; (b) conditionalities attached to development

assistance and admission into international organizations; and (c) empowered citizens who make claims against states and international institutions that often echo (d) minimal standards of human rights.[4]

However, others maintain that such interventions and restrictions on state autonomy have not gone far enough and that human rights and economic and religious freedoms need to be applied more vigorously and thoroughly in a manner that would trump principles of state autonomy and non-intervention. This view is perhaps most evident in the discussion surrounding humanitarian interventions and the idea of responsibility to protect. It has encouraged a more solidarist approach to international society, if not a desire to create a world society. Such views are, in part, an acknowledgement of developments in the arenas of globalisation and human security. They also reflect shifting normative concerns. Regardless of their origin they raise important questions about the nature and desirability of pluralism and the substantive content of the rules and institutions in existence among the state members of international society.

Hedley Bull first raised many of these same concerns in *The Anarchical Society* when he distinguished between pluralist and solidarist accounts of international society.[5] Bull's distinction rested on the normative content of the rules and institutions that demarcated international society and the degree to which they gave priority to order among states and the sovereign rights of these states as opposed to more substantive values such as human rights or justice that would limit these states' rights. Barry Buzan in reiterating the significance of these issues for the English School has also stressed that the pluralist–solidarist discussion is one that takes place within an interstate international society.[6] Bull, for his part, urged caution in adopting more solidarist approaches less they fail to reflect a consensus among all members of the society of states.[7] This more cautious view has been shared and reiterated by Robert Jackson in part, in response to the interventions of the 1990s.[8] Yet Bull also expressed concern about resistance to an order imposed with Western values that failed to acknowledge the concerns of many peoples and states with matters of recognition, economic justice, and cultural autonomy.[9] Others, including Nicholas Wheeler and Andrew Linklater, have taken up the solidarist position emphasising themes of justice and human security and defending interventionist practices.[10]

The concern for human rights and human security that has been encouraged by developments both within and among states suggests a significant normative shift for international society as it extends the subjects of international society to include individuals and creates a tension between the state and other agents for the protection of these individuals. Much of this concern was evident in the alleged ascendancy of liberal values in the aftermath of the Cold War. Within English School accounts, much attention has been given to the discourse and practice of human security and responsibility to protect as evidence of this turn towards solidarism.[11] The attention to human rights has been important in shedding light on abuses and strengthening the standards against which the practices of states are assessed. Yet as Jennifer Welsh reminds us and in spite of some hopes that this normative shift would lead to numerous interventions, such occurrences have been limited.[12] While the promotion of these values and practices occurred both within and outside of regional and international institutions they have largely reflected the hegemonic position of the United States and a certain hubris shared by many of its allies. Additionally, none of this activity has moved very far from the particular interests of these states, as became clearer in the wake of the terrorist attacks on the United States in 2001. Normative considerations gave way to security interests and what appeared to be a more solidarist international society or even emergent world society, returned to something which at best represented a pluralist international society of sovereign states, and at worst a new imperial order.

In spite of former UN secretary general Kofi Annan's claim that the aim of the UN Charter must be to protect individual human beings, it is clear that it lacks the capacity to do so on any sustainable basis. It is also clear that there is as yet no consensus among states about how best to do this. This has led to suggestions, such as that of Allan Buchanan and Robert Keohane, for legitimating alternative and more exclusive mechanisms for intervention.[13] Such alternatives, however, present a challenge to international society especially as they tend to serve the interests of more powerful states as much as they might solidarist values. Thus while the interventions of individual states and collectivities such as NATO have been designed to provide a degree of protection for individuals facing harm in places such as Kosovo and Libya, these have been undertaken at the lowest possible risk and cost to the intervening party and in the absence of any consideration of the longer-term and multidimensional needs of the populations involved.[14] Additionally, the diplomatic activity surrounding this increased activity has yet to demonstrate a deep commitment in support of an inclusive consensus. This is reminiscent of the exclusionary practices of European governments in the late nineteenth century, so thoroughly analysed and critiqued by Cemil Aydin.[15] At that time, Western powers, in their eagerness to impose standards of civilisation often riddled with racial and cultural biases, failed to acknowledge the extent to which non-Western states were seeking legitimacy and recognition so that they could participate more fully in international society. Instead, then as today, the concerns of these dominant powers have often reflected their own particular interests. From an English School perspective, attention to the practice of states and to the intention of those who Jackson describes as the diplomatic community is critically important in examining the substantive character of international society.

The arena of economic globalisation, while less widely discussed within the English School literature, is also of interest, for here there is much greater evidence of a body of substantive rules and a more robust governance framework in the form of the institutionalisation of these rules embodied, for example, in the European Union and the World Trade Organization.[16] In this arena as well, the commitment to a common set of values and practices is often compromised in response to local or national interests. Member governments regularly and repeatedly seek exemptions to rules or behave in ways that reflect a stronger commitment to local interests over shared values. Additionally, the significant transition in the international distribution of economic power with the emergence of more active and influential emerging powers, including China, India, and Brazil, has added a new set of interests and values into the governance process that has only partially been reflected in changes to governance structures and decision-making councils. It would seem from the diplomacy of these states in arenas including the UN Security Council and the World Trade Organization that their interests and aspirations for international order are not incompatible with a pluralist international society, even as they differ over some substantive values.[17] To ignore differences over substantive values in an effort to construct a solidarist international society that entrenched cosmopolitan principles at the risk of alienating these emerging powers might impede an opportunity to strengthen the fabric of a vibrant pluralistic international society.

In contemplating the future balance between a more pluralist or solidarist international society, attention to the practice of individual states is of critical importance. Welsh, and R.J. Vincent before her, remind us that state practice provides the clearest reading on the acceptability and meaning of these solidarist principles that have become more commonplace in contemporary international society. State practice may reveal a profound level of scepticism towards principles that impede the sovereign authority of their own national governments to resist the homogenising practices of entities such as the EU and the WTO or from a NATO vision of R2P that they seek to impose on others. Often the pressures for solidarist values emanate from dominant powers with less regard for the concerns of lesser powers and with the ability to reject such values when desired. Such practices have reinforced the view that international society is inherently Eurocentric and has failed to adapt to a truly international society. Continuing such practices carries the risk that a normative concern with a progressive agenda gets diluted with national interests and hijacked by power considerations such that a move towards economic or political justice becomes the latest iteration of imperialism.

A truly inclusive form of pluralism needs to recognise and legitimise the autonomous rights and culture of different communities. In view of such a possibility, support for a more pluralist international society is understandable. Failure to move in this direction poses a risk to the advances that have been made through international society. This was indeed Bull's primary concern. As Welsh notes, it was also a concern for Vincent, even as he tried to extrapolate a more responsive approach to human rights. 'In the end, he could not accept a normative approach to international relations that would allow the strong— who were both "untrusted and untrustworthy"—to impose justice as they understood it.'[18] Perhaps this lies at the root of concerns about the future direction of a more solidarist international society. Alex Bellamy and Matt McDonald maintain that 'the key challenge' for English School proponents of a more solidarist approach 'is whether practices of security can emerge that are sufficiently solidarist to have real impact [...] whilst sufficiently pluralist to meet Hedley Bull's concerns about the dangers of undermining international order.'[19]

The dilemma that confronts the globe is the difficulty in overcoming states' interests to devise programmes of progressive change to address the problems emanating from environmental degradation, economic inequalities, and identity politics, balanced against relying on seemingly more 'universal' approaches that are primarily imperial projects serving the interests of dominant powers. Hurrell is right to stress the limitations of a state-based pluralism as the world confronts the myriad of problems involved in managing the environment, the global economy and its plurality of identities. To identify the limitations is not to offer an acceptable alternative. The states that comprise international society show little inclination to move along a common path to a more effective governance of the existing global order. There are few signs that powerful states are going to abandon their privilege and interests easily. It remains necessary to recognise the continued importance of state-based diplomacy and state-supported order to make the necessary transition to the more effective governance that these modern challenges demand. As Turan Kayaoglu writes in his critique of the Eurocentric character of parts of the English School, such an effort must be truly pluralistic:

> By acknowledging the importance of the values, norms, and institutions that states share, and theorizing how values, norms, and institutions shape international relations, the English School has advanced our understanding of international relations and created a vision for a more stable and peaceful international system. However, the commitment of English School scholars to the Westphalian narrative prevents them both from exploring the contribution of non-Western normative and historical sources adequately, apart

from passing references to these contributions, and from theorizing about cross-cultural interactions in contemporary international relations.[20]

An international society rooted in a more inclusive form of pluralism that gets over its Eurocentric biases has the opportunity to offer a path through diplomacy and institutionalised consensus building to constrain the dominance of power and national interests and move, however incrementally, towards addressing some of these concerns. The pluralist cornerstone, one that respects and protects state sovereignty even as it acknowledges the enhanced concern for rights or the shifting demands for a more integrated global economy, remains a critical foundation for international society.

Notes

1. Barry Buzan, *From International to World Society: English School Theory and the Social Structure of Globalization* (Cambridge: Cambridge University Press, 2004).
2. Turan Kayaoglu, 'Westphalian Eurocentrism in International Relations Theory', *International Studies Review* 12 (2010), 193–217.
3. Andrew Hurrell, *On Global Order: Power, Values, and the Constitution of International Society* (Oxford: Oxford University Press, 2007), 297.
4. Matthew, S. Weinert, 'Reframing the Pluralist-Solidarist Debate', *Millennium* 40:1 (2011), 33.
5. Hedley Bull, 'The Grotian Conception of International Society' in *Diplomatic Investigations: Essays in the Theory of International Politics*, eds Martin Wight and Hubert Butterfield (London: Allen & Unwin, 1966).
6. Buzan, *From International to World Society*, 139.
7. Hedley Bull, *The Anarchical Society* (London: Macmillan, 1977), 157.
8. Robert Jackson, T*he Global Covenant: Human Conduct in a World of States* (Oxford: Oxford University Press, 2000).
9. Hedley Bull, 'The Revolt against the West' in *The Expansion of International Society*, eds Hedley Bull and Adam Watson (New York: Oxford University Press, 1985), 217-28.
10. Nicholas Wheeler, *Saving Strangers: Humanitarian Intervention in International Society* (Oxford: Oxford University Press, 2000); Andrew Linklater, *The Transformation of Political Community* (London: Macmillan, 1998).
11. Wheeler provides among the most extensive discussions in his *Saving Strangers*; also see Alex J. Bellamy and Matt McDonald, 'Securing International Society: Towards an English School Discourse of Security', *Australian Journal of Political Science* 39:2 (2004), 307-24.
12. Jennifer Welsh, 'A normative case for pluralism: reassessing Vincent's views on humanitarian intervention', *International Affairs* 87:5 (2011), 1193-204.
13. Allen Buchanan and Robert O. Keohane, 'The Preventive Use of Force: A Cosmopolitan Institutional Proposal', *Ethics and International Affairs* 18:1 (2004), 1-22.
14. Aidan Hehir and Robert Murray, eds *Libya, The Responsibility to Protect and the Future of Humanitarian Intervention* (Houndmills: Palgrave Macmillan, 2013).
15. Cemil Aydin, *The Politics of Anti-Westernism in Asia* (New York: Columbia University

Press, 2007).

16. Barry Buzan, 'International Political Economy and Globalisation', in *International Society and Its Critics*, ed. Alex J. Bellamy (Oxford: Oxford University Press, 2004), 115-34.

17. See, for example, Rosemary Foot and Andrew Walker, *China, the United States, and Global Order* (Cambridge: Cambridge University Press, 2011); Shogo Suzuki, 'Seeking "Legitimate" Great Power Status in the Post-Cold War International Society: China's and Japan's Participation in UNPKO', *International Relations* 22:1 (2008), 45-63; Jonathan E. Davis, 'From Ideology to Pragmatism: China's Position on Humanitarian Intervention in the Post-Cold War Era', *Vanderbilt Journal of Transnational Law* 44:2 (2011), 217-83; Allen Carlson, 'Moving Beyond Sovereignty?' *Journal of Contemporary China* 20:68 (2011), 89-102.

18. R.J. Vincent cited in Jennifer Welsh, 'A Normative Case for pluralism: Reassessing Vincent's Views on Humanitarian Intervention', *International Affairs* 87:5 (2011), 1202; see also R.J. Vincent, *Human Rights and International Relations* (Cambridge: Cambridge University Press, 1986).

19. Bellamy and McDonald, 'Securing International Society: Towards an English School Discourse of Security', 309.

20. Kayaoglu, 'Westphalian Eurocentrism', 209.

14

Pluralism, the English School and the Challenge of Normative Theory

JOHN WILLIAMS
DURHAM UNIVERSITY, UK

The pluralist position within the English School is typically associated with an account of international society that stresses three principal features: the centrality of inter-state consensus to international order, the significance of ethical diversity (or pluralism) amongst states, and the fragility of normative progress. This chapter aims to explain and challenge each of these features and to outline an alternative version of the pluralist position that retains key English School claims whilst arguing in favour of the potential insights available from reorientating analysis towards a subaltern perspective on politics as an important element of a normatively rich version of pluralism.

To turn to the first two of those pluralist characteristics, pluralist accounts of international society derive from essentially empirical claims: that international society's principal members are states which have, through historical interaction and experience reached consensus around certain norms and principles of behaviour sufficient to sustain order amongst themselves.[1] This process, the standard account continues, has been significantly affected by the fact of great diversity in ethical principles and schemas within and across political communities. As a result, the third claim follows: the consensus amongst diverse states that sustains order is a fragile one and seeking to push it in any specific 'progressive' direction is a dangerous course of action. This account is most typically associated with Hedley Bull, James Mayall and Robert Jackson as leading exemplars of the pluralist position.[2]

This account reflects many of the virtues of the English School's approach to theorising international relations. The first two claims draw heavily on the English School's extensive interest in and work on the historical development of international societies, exemplified in a number of landmark volumes.[3] This historical interest is also reflected in the contribution of English School scholars to understanding the institutions that manifest particular historical instances of international societies. Such institutions, understood as settled and durable social practices that help to constitute actors, frame practices and enable assessment of action in specific issue areas, have emerged as a major theme of contemporary English School scholarship.[4] Such institutional constellations are historically dynamic, and therefore understanding the processes through which they change is an important empirical research project within the English school, and one with significant implications for normative analysis, too. This significance includes the idea of their fragility as a result of the historically specific and consensually based nature of such institutions.

The engagement between international society and the nature, development and effectiveness of international law as one institution of international society has greatly influenced English School efforts to formalise an account of 'pluralism' and 'solidarism' as distinct intellectual positions. Both labels originate in an assessment of the extent to which law enforcement takes place.[5] This has subsequently extended into the dominant contemporary understanding, rooted in the idea and ideal of 'solidarism' as a cosmopolitan ethic predicated on a universal human community rooted in the universal moral significance of each individual, such that international law and its enforcement is an extension of cosmopolitan, even 'natural', rights possessed by all humans. This most commonly manifests itself in a commitment to universal human rights of the sort associated with landmark international declarations, treaties and covenants as the most politically prominent and theoretically dominant version of such cosmopolitanism. The English school's path to this form of solidarism is, characteristically, indebted to its engagement with changing historical context and circumstance, most importantly the development of debates over the nature of a post-Cold War international order and especially the emergence of intense debate about humanitarian intervention. In this arena, work by English School writers such as Andrew Linklater on political order and Nicholas Wheeler on humanitarian intervention proved to be influential well beyond the realms of the English School.[6] The claim to offer a progressive account of not only how international society was developing but also how it ought to continue to develop appeared to have been passed to a liberal solidarism not just better able to capture the normative aspirations of the post-Cold War decade but also far more attuned to deep-rooted structural changes in world politics being wrought by globalisation and the challenge to the English School's state-centrism.[7]

The transition from Bull's empirical assessment of the extent of consensus on the enforcement of international law to a far more self-consciously normative proposition is a path that pluralism has not followed to anything like the same extent. The best-known contemporary restatement of the pluralist cause, Robert Jackson's *The Global Covenant* remains rooted in the empirical claims about the historical evolution of inter-state consensus under conditions of ethical diversity I highlighted at the outset, with the same normative conclusion about the fragility of interstate order and thus the need for extreme caution in advocating alterations that cannot be demonstrably rooted in interstate consensus. Jackson's neglect of non-state forms of politics and political economy and resistance to cosmopolitan ethical propositions is striking.[8] This led Andrew Hurrell to argue for the abandonment of the pluralist position as normatively viable within the English School, even though it may retain some analytical utility in accounting for the behaviour of non-liberal states.[9] This analytical value has arguably increased subsequently, given the push-back against the liberal trajectory of the 1990s by established and emerging world powers such as Russia, China and India. The debates over the concept of Responsibility to Protect – arguably the high-water mark of liberal solidarist interventionism when launched in 2001 and subject to critique, resistance and reformulation, or even outright rejection, by Russia, China and many post-colonial states in the period since – is instructive in this regard.[10]

This persistent empiricism inevitably and unavoidably hampers pluralism's normative dimension and stifles the possibility of a more ambitious normative agenda. Paradoxically, this comes at the expense of pluralism's ostensible interest in ethical diversity. By reducing ethical diversity to that manifest amongst the world's states and by seeing this phenomenon as an empirical fact about the world, pluralism of the sort typically associated with the English School is only able to offer a normative assessment of the *consequences* of the existence of ethically diverse states, it cannot offer a properly normative defence of the value to be found in such diversity itself.

Developing a pluralist account predicated on the desirability of ethical diversity in the world holds out the potential for pluralism to follow the path of solidarism towards becoming a more fully developed normative theory of international relations. In parallel with solidarism's commitment to ethical cosmopolitanism, usually via human rights, pluralism can offer an account of the ethical significance of diversity. Achieving this requires substantial development of some of the philosophical and methodological claims that are usually associated, although often only implicitly, with the pluralist position in the English School.[11] Pluralism's empirical proclivities are manifest in its rather uncertain, and unsatisfactory, methodological stance. Often associated with what Bull[12] described as a 'classical approach', something restated by

Jackson,[13] this produces scepticism of formal methodologies, whether those associated with positivism or with philosophically oriented approaches to ethics.[14] In Bull's case in particular, this latter was also aligned with a high degree of moral scepticism, such that claims to access to moral truth or truths, and the means by which such access could be gained, was treated with considerable suspicion.[15]

Overcoming moral scepticism and an empirical view dominated by an international society of states at a time when the transformations of world politics wrought by globalisation have dramatically extended the range of actors important to world politics is imperative to the future of a pluralist stance. Fortunately, there is much to commend the opportunities this offers, in terms of the theoretical development of the English School and the analytical insights, both empirical and normative, that are potentially available. Key to this is the recognition that ethical diversity is only loosely linked to statehood, and while pluralists have long accepted that the diversity of states is a poor facsimile of the wealth of human communities and their diversity, its overwhelming commitment to the centrality of states to international relations and the necessity of preserving interstate consensus around rules and norms of state conduct have precluded any serious engagement with the full panoply of ethical diversity. An openness to human communities as the source of ethical diversity connects pluralism to engaging with a world politics unshackled from international society and enables it to better embrace the importance of the transnational and world society dimensions of the English School's theorising of international relations.[16] Further, a focus on community means that pluralism offers a way to recognise one of the most important features – analytically and normatively – of contemporary world politics: the complex interplay in human politics of simultaneous multiple community memberships, often establishing competing or even irreconcilable normative demands.[17]

This is not to dismiss the durability of international society and its normative agenda – pluralism's traditional arena of enquiry – but is to locate that within a far more diverse arena of world politics such that sub-state, non-state and transnational actors can be accommodated and the role they play in shaping ethical debate about how to live in a complex world can be analysed.[18] Seeing community as the key analytical level for theorising ethical diversity enables pluralism to encompass the multiplicity of ethical schemas that help to constitute individuals through their multiple community memberships, it also generates the potential for establishing within pluralism a distinctive ethical perspective to challenge its characterisation as conservative, even regressive.

Central to this claim for the potential for a progressive pluralist position is an argument derived from the origins of the subaltern studies historiographical movement, associated initially with historians of the Indian sub-continent.[19] One of the most interesting aspects of that work, redolent of its indebtedness to an intellectual tradition that traces its origins back through Gramsci to Marx, is the powerful claim that understanding power structures is best achieved from the perspectives of the victims of such structures.[20] This, too, challenges the normal pluralist perspective, which typically heavily privileges political elites and their perspective on the ethical challenges of maintaining the rules and norms of international society and its institutions.[21] This creates a critical edge to pluralism that Hurrell,[22] for example, regarded as blunted beyond repair and creates the conditions whereby the productive theoretical tension between pluralism and solidarism, which had run into the sands of ostensible incommensurability and pluralism's normative theoretical inadequacies, can once again contribute positively to the development of English School theory.

English School pluralism need not deserve its current reputation as a statist, conservative and declining facet of the English School project, retaining only some analytical utility in relation to the behaviour of some states within international society. What ought to be the core normative claim of a pluralist position – that the ethical diversity of human communities is to be valued and championed – can be recovered from the empiricism and moral scepticism of its post-Bull agenda. To do so requires substantial revision to pluralism's methodology and a far-reaching reorientation of its analytical focus towards communities, in their diversity, multiplicity and continuing interaction through individuals' multiple memberships. The costs involved, however, are repaid by the opportunity to re-establish pluralism as a vital contributor to the English School's distinctive theoretical ambition to offer analytical insight and normative evaluation of a world politics that goes far beyond the inter-state.

Notes

1.   Hedley Bull, *The Anarchical Society: A Study of Order in World Politics* (London: Macmillan, 1977), 13.
2.   Bull, *The Anarchical Society*; James Mayall, *World Politics: Progress and Its Limits* (Cambridge: Polity, 2000); Robert H. Jackson, *The Global Covenant: Human Conduct in a World of States* (Oxford: Oxford University Press, 2000); Barry Buzan, *An Introduction to the English School of International Relations: the Societal Approach* (Cambridge: Polity, 2014), 89-112.
3.   Hedley Bull and Adam Watson, eds, *The Expansion of International Society* (Oxford: Clarendon Press, 1984); Adam Watson, *The Evolution of International Society: a Comparative Historical Analysis* (London: Routledge, 1992); Barry Buzan and Richard Little, *International Systems in World History: Remaking the Study of International Relations* (Oxford: Oxford University Press, 2000); Edward Keene, *Beyond the Anarchical Society: Grotius, Colonialism and Order in World Politics* (Cambridge:

Cambridge University Press, 2002).

4. Barry Buzan, *From International to World Society? English School Theory and the Social Structure of Globalization* (Cambridge: Cambridge University Press, 2004); Laust Schouenborg, 'A New Institutionalism? The English School as International Sociological Theory', *International Relations* 25:1 (2011), 26-44; Kilian Spandler, 'The Political International Society: Change in Primary and Secondary Institutions', *Review of International Studies* 41:3 (2015), 601-22.

5. Hedley Bull, 'The Grotian Conception of International Society', in *Hedley Bull on International Society*, eds Kai Alderson and Andrew Hurrell (Basingstoke: Macmillan, 2000).

6. Andrew Linklater, *The Transformation of Political Community: Ethical Foundations for a Post-Westphalian Era* (Cambridge: Polity, 1998); Nicholas J. Wheeler, *Saving Strangers: Humanitarian Intervention in International Society* (Oxford: Oxford University Press, 2000).

7. John Williams, 'Pluralism, Solidarism and the Emergence of World Society in English School Theory', *International Relations* 19:1 (2005), 19-38.

8. Jackson, *The Global Covenant.*

9. Andrew Hurrell, *On Global Order: Power, Values, and the Constitution of International Society* (Oxford: Oxford University Press, 2007), 292.

10. E.g. Alex Bellamy, *Responsibility to Protect: a Defence* (Oxford: Oxford University Press, 2014).

11. John Williams, *Ethics, Diversity and World Politics: Saving Pluralism From Itself?* (Oxford: Oxford University Press, 2015), 36-110.

12. Hedley Bull, 'International Theory: The Case for the Classical Approach', *World Politics* 18:3 (1966), 361-77.

13. Jackson, *The Global Covenant*, 44-96.

14. E.g. James Mayall, 'The Limits of Progress: Normative Reasoning in the English School', in *Theorising International Society: English School Methods*, ed. Cornelia Navari (Basingstoke: Palgrave Macmillan, 2009), 209.

15. Renee Jeffery, 'Australian Realism and International Relations: John Anderson and Hedley Bull on Ethics, Religion and Society', *International Politics* 45:1 (2008), 52-71; John Williams, 'Hedley Bull and Just War: Missed Opportunities and Lessons to be Learned', *European Journal of International Relations* 16:2 (2011), 179-96.

16. Buzan, *From International to World Society?*

17. Williams, *Ethics, Diversity and World Politics.*

18. Ibid., 111-48.

19. E.g. Ranajit Guha and Gayatri Chakravorty Spivak, *Selected Subaltern Studies* (Oxford: Oxford University Press, 1988).

20. Williams, *Ethics, Diversity and World Politics,* 124-34.

21. Jackson, *The Global Covenant,* 134; Peter Wilson, 'The English School Meets the Chicago School: The Case for a Grounded Theory of International Institutions', *International Studies Review* 14:4 (2012), 567-90.

22. Hurrell, *On Global Order,* 292.

15

Great Power Management: English School Meets Governmentality?

ALEXANDER ASTROV

CENTRAL EUROPEAN UNIVERSITY, HUNGARY

There is a puzzling and, as far as I can see, unnoticed discontinuity between the five major institutions of international society identified by Hedley Bull. Four of them – war, diplomacy, international law and the balance of power – are hardly Bull's own inventions. One can argue about the exact meaning of 'war' or the 'balance of power' within the English School framework, but there is hardly any doubt as to the existence of the phenomena defined by these terms. This is not the case with the fifth institution: great power management. It is not immediately clear at all what the term can possibly stand for in practice; especially so if we take 'management' to be more than just a word and assign some analytical value to it. But then what exactly this value should be?

Bull himself provides little help here, and until recently, 'great power management' received little attention from subsequent generations of the English School, certainly much less than the other four institutions. This, I believe, is due neither to simple theoretical negligence, nor to the demise of great powers, but results from the difficulty in reconciling the practice of great power management with one of the major tenets of the English School; namely, its insistence on avoiding 'domestic analogy'.[1] Contrary to Martin Wight's argument, understanding international system by analogy with the state was practiced not only by international lawyers and confused theorists.[2] This is how the great powers of the nineteenth century understood themselves. With one important qualification: by the time such understanding was articulated, the state itself was no longer understood in terms of the classical Hobbesian opposition of the commonwealth and the state of nature. The term 'management' is not after all Bull's theoretical invention, but appears instead precisely in this practical articulation by the great powers themselves in reference to the procedures established at the Congress of Vienna:

> The advantage of this mode of proceeding is that you treat [other states] as a body with early and becoming respect. You keep the power by concert and management in your own hands, but without openly assuming authority to their exclusion. You obtain a sort of sanction from them for what you are determined at all events to do, which they cannot well withhold ... . And you entitle yourselves, without disrespect to them, to meet together for dispatch of business for an indefinite time to their exclusion.[3]

Only the authorship of Castlereagh and the context of the international congress betray the fact that this statement was made on behalf of the European great powers and not some European executive. Moreover, the familiar 'domestic' division of powers between the executive and the legislator is clearly echoed here in the distinction between 'management' and 'power by concert'.

Note, that only a century or so earlier, the distinction between the great powers and the rest is drawn differently, by the English ambassador to the Netherlands, William Temple, for example: in terms of the Aristotelian forms of government rather than modern division of powers, and the 'managerial' stance of the lesser states, referred to as 'tradesmen', is not only opposed to the 'aristocratic' posture of the great powers but treated somewhat disparagingly.[4] These changes parallel historic developments *within* European states, and it is possible to suggest that the victors in the Napoleonic wars recognised in the French undertaking not only a very old ambition to impose upon Europe a single *authority*, but also a genuinely new one: to establish a European *government*.[5] And while resolutely rejecting the former, they stealthily embraced the latter. Hence 'power by concert' and 'management' in the hands of the few, now recognised as 'great' in some distinctly new way; but still, as with the earlier 'aristocracy'/'tradesmen' distinction, by analogy with the historically specific ordering of the state.

In Bull, unlike in American realism, great powers are such not merely because of their material capabilities, but also 'by right'. However, in order to avoid domestic analogy, he prefers to conceptualise this right not in terms of 'ruling' – either aristocratic or executive – but by reference to specifically 'international' practices and institutions. Thus, 'great powers manage their relations with one another in the interest of international order', not least by preserving the general balance of power, or they 'exploit their preponderance in relation to the rest of the international society', by acting either in concert or unilaterally.[6] Yet, this results in theoretical confusion. Either, in the case of the relations between great powers, great power management becomes indistinguishable from the balance of power; or, in the case of their relations with lesser states, international society becomes indistinguishable from the realist international system shaped by the distribution of material capabilities.

Not surprisingly then, later attempts at clarifying the nature of the great powers' rights effectively re-introduced domestic analogy, but in two distinct ways. First, Ian Clark started with the acceptance of Bull's point that international society, while being shaped by great powers, is also the condition of possibility for their very existence (as with the other four institutions), so that 'the absence of a great-power directorate entails the demise of international society altogether'.[7] Yet, since the principle of consent underpinning the existence of the great power directorate is limited to the great powers themselves, they effectively occupy the position of a (quasi) sovereign within international society.[8]

The second, more recent, line of argument proceeds not by establishing affinity between great power management and 'classical' sovereign authority but by questioning the juridical theory of sovereignty as such. On this view, lawyers and theorists criticised by Wight were mistaken not so much in projecting domestic sovereignty onto the international system but in their understanding of domestic sovereignty in the first place. This line of argument finds its inspiration in the writings of Michel Foucault, where the rise of Westphalian system is marked not only with further development of such 'political-military' instruments as war, diplomacy and the balance of power, but also with the emergence of a new instrument – 'a permanent military apparatus' which required a totally new hold on state's own power, but also the new means of control over power-management by other states.[9] This new form of power-management, both domestically and internationally, is called 'police', which from the seventeenth century 'begins to refer to the set of means by which the state's forces can be increased while preserving the state in good order.' And since in the newly created Westphalian order 'there will be imbalance if within the European equilibrium there is a state, not my state, with bad police', action must be taken in the name of the balance of power so that 'there is good police, even in other states'.[10]

Note that in this formulation, great power management, although closely linked with the balance of power, is distinct from it. Also, as a mode of managing the balance of power and international society as a whole, it is neither limited to the concert of great powers, nor takes the form of the exploitation of their material preponderance vis-à-vis lesser states. In fact, over time, 'police' develops into explicitly liberal 'conduct of conduct' of individuals domestically and states internationally; an activity distinguished by its ambition to conduct the conduct of individuals/states themselves recognised as capable of freely conducting their own activities.

The crucial aspect of this mode of power-management extensively explored by governmentality literature in IR generally and in security studies in particular, is that 'governors' here represent entities whose power 'is not political power at all, but purely administrative power – power of the experts and interpreters of life'.[11] At first sight, this seems to suggest that analytical and practical distinction between 'management' and other institutions identified by both Bull and Foucault as explicitly 'political' comes at the expense of 'greatness'. There is hardly anything 'great' about the managerial pursuits of even the most powerful states, not only willingly assuming the role of global administrators but also often transferring this role to private agencies. By demoting states to the position of administrators, 'police' management does not merely modify the restriction on the membership in the great powers club, but tends to consign the establishment as such to the 'waste bin of history'; hence, the array of euphemisms, from the 'leader' to 'indispensable nation', recently introduced by the US in its self-acclamations.[12]

Still, as always, the situation may well be more complex and ambivalent. After all, underpinning the 'police' expertise over life is a prior distinction familiar to liberalism from the very beginning: between those who, being capable of free conduct themselves, can be governed in this manner and those who, because of their ignorance of or aversion to liberal conception of freedom, can only be governed in some other way.[13] And this distinction remains resolutely political. The problem – or, rather, one of the many theoretical and practical challenges here – is that this explicitly political decision is no longer the sole prerogative of the state, even the most powerful ones. Various non-governmental agencies, especially those concerned with representing the whole of humanity, are identifying the sins of the world by offering their interpretations of life, while leaving to the states, as their 'secular wing' the managerial task of actually addressing the problems.[14] Consequently, it is not at all impossible to imagine a world in which something like 'great power management' is clearly at work, while 'greatness', 'power' and 'management' can no longer be unproblematically clustered together and allocated to single entity.

Notes

1. See Hidemi Suganami, *The Domestic Analogy and World Order Proposals* (Cambridge: Cambridge University Press, 1989).
2. Martin Wight, 'Why is there no International Theory?' *International Relations* 2:1 (April 1960), 35-48.
3. Gerry J. Simpson, *Great Powers and Outlaw States: Unequal Sovereigns in the International Legal Order* (Cambridge: Cambridge University Press, 2004), 99.
4. Istvan Hont, 'Free Trade and the Economic Limits to National Politics: Neo-Machiavellian Political Economy Reconsidered', *The Economic Limits to Modern Politics* (Cambridge: Cambridge University Press, 1990).
5. Paul Schroeder, 'Historical Reality vs Neorealist Theory', *International Security* 19:1 (1994), 108-48.
6. Hedley Bull, *The Anarchical Society: A Study in World Politics* (London: Macmillan Press, 1977), 205-6.
7. Ian Clark, *Hegemony in International Society* (Oxford: Oxford University Press, 2011), 37.
8. Ian Clark, *International Legitimacy and World Society* (Oxford: Oxford University Press, 2007), 101-2.
9. Michel Foucault, *Security, Territory, Population: Lectures at the Collègede France, 1977–1978* (Basingstoke: Palgrave Macmillan, 2007), 305-6.
10. Ibid., 313-15. Within the English School, see Iver Neumann and Ole Jacob Sending, *Governing the Global Polity: Practice, Mentality, Rationality* (University of Michigan Press, 2010).
11. Mika Ojakangas, 'Impossible Dialogue on Biopower: Agamben and Foucault', *Foucault Studies* 2 (2005), 16.
12. Richard Ned Lebow and Robert Kelly, 'Thucydides and Hegemony: Athens and the United States', *Review of International Studies* 27:4 (October 2001), 606.
13. Barry Hindess, 'Politics as Government: Michel Foucault's Analysis of Political Reason', *Alternatives: Global, Local, Political* 30:4 (2005), 389-413.
14. Michael Hardt and Antonio Negri, *Empire* (Cambridge: Harvard University Press, 2000), 36.

16

The Need for an English School Research Programme

ROBERT W. MURRAY

FRONTIER CENTRE FOR PUBLIC POLICY AND UNIVERSITY OF ALBERTA, CANADA

Traditionally, the English School (ES) approach to international relations has not been overly concerned with typically American social science interest in methods and empirical testing. As Cornelia Navari notes in this volume, early ES scholars preferred to focus their attention on participant observation as opposed to structure, system or causational variables. It is this lack of methodological rigor that has hindered the development of the ES as a sufficiently empirical *theory* of international relations, and one that should be addressed in order to substantially increase the School's explanatory power in modern international relations theory.

A major problem facing the School's ability to be tested as a *theory* in the social science tradition is the lack of concern with methods and a clear framework by which one could determine whether a scholar was, or was not, using a distinctly English School approach. Dale Copeland effectively summarises a definite gap in ES thought: 'Without knowing clearly what it is that is being explained, there is simply no way of gathering evidence to support or disconfirm a particular [English School] author's position.'[1] This is not to say that ES scholarship should adhere to the strict positivist standards imposed by American social science at all, but there is validity in saying there are too few commonalities between ES writers to define it as a coherent theoretical lens.[2] Richard Little, building on an argument first presented by Buzan, claims that there are at least three distinct ways to view the School:

> ES theory may be considered first as a set of ideas to be
> found in the minds of statesmen; second, as a set of ideas to

be found in the minds of political theorists; and third, as a set of externally imposed concepts that define the material and social structures of the international system.[3]

Further, some ES writers have attempted to cast the School as more valuable because of its methodological openness and critical possibilities. For instance, Roger Epp argues:

> In other words, the English school recollects a tradition – the historicality of open-ended, intersecting, competing narratives – *within* which critical resources are already present. Its erudite, generous horizons contain what amount to enabling prejudices: the biases of openness to an indeterminate future.[4]

Even so, the lack of any identifiable hard-core assumptions or foundational principles makes theoretical evaluation of the School and its empirical validity virtually impossible.

Among the main reasons for the School's lack of attention in mainstream international theory is the inability of scholars to test the tenets of the ES, to identify exactly when it can be a said a scholar is using the school (and not casually just referring to a society of states), and more importantly, evaluating whether the ongoing body of literature that falls under an ES schema is providing novel contributions, or if the more current conceptions of the School since its reorganisation are actually falsifying what early thinkers like Butterfield, Wight, Bull and Vincent had in mind.[5] In order to address such theoretical looseness, there may be value in attempting to impose methodological rigour to the School.

Perhaps the ideal approach to formulating a more rigorous conception of the ES can be found in the works of Imre Lakatos. In many ways, Lakatos' work on Scientific Research Programmes tries to do exactly what early School thinkers sought to accomplish from the outset – to find a middle ground between two competing theories (in Lakatos' case between Popper and Kuhn) that both had relevance, but fell short in any kind of *truth*.[6] For Lakatos, the challenge was providing a way to balance the claims made by Karl Popper on one hand and Thomas Kuhn on the other. Lakatos' contribution to metatheoretical evaluation is a method of determining the novelty of theory and whether contributions actually add value, or ultimately degenerate, the hard-core assumptions of a hypothesis. The driving concern for Lakatos was to determine when one scientific theory should replace another. Lakatos saw Popper's views as too dependent upon falsification and a view of science as too open to dissent:

> [Popper] still construes falsification as the result of a duel between theory and observation, without another, better theory necessarily being involved. The real Popper has never explained in detail the appeal procedure by which some accepted basic statements may be eliminated.[7]

Kuhn's theory, on the other hand, was far too subjective for Lakatos, as Kuhn believed that science was what the powers at large thought it was:

> Kuhn certainly showed that the psychology of science can reveal important and, indeed, sad truths. But the psychology of science is not autonomous; for the-rationally reconstructed-growth of science takes place essentially in the world of ideas, in Plato's and Popper's third world, in the world of articulated knowledge which is independent of knowing subjects.[8]

As a result, Lakatos sought to 'develop a theory of scientific method which was sufficiently subtle to cope with the detail of the actual history of science and yet sufficiently rationalistic to resist the political dangers presented by Kuhn'.[9] This endeavour on the part of Lakatos led to the development of his scientific research programme method. This method consists of four primary components, namely a hard core, a negative heuristic, a positive heuristic and a protective belt of auxiliary hypotheses. According to Lakatosian logic, a theory is not dismissed based on falsification alone, but is instead evaluated as a series of contributions that either provide novel facts to a research programme, or may instead lead to the creation of a new one.

Evaluating theory in the Lakatosian sense requires the substantiation of empirical facts, however, which is an ongoing flaw in English School work (especially when examining world society arguments). Lakatos claims:

> The time-honoured empirical criterion for a satisfactory theory was agreement with the observed facts. Our empirical criterion for a series of theories is that it should produce new facts. *The idea of growth and the concept of empirical character are soldiered into one.*[10]

Within ES circles, the need to empirically verify theoretical contributions tends to be ignored.[11] Instead, English School approaches prefer to favour rationalist methods that highlight the evolution of international societies throughout human history. Unfortunately, even this claim to historical explanation by ES writers is interpreted as weak. 'For a school that prides itself on offering a historical approach to international relations, there are surprisingly few diplomatic-historical analyses that extensively utilise archival sources or documentary collections.'[12] Beyond the lack of empirical content of ES theory, even the use of historical explanation is questioned in terms of what the school is trying to do through its work.[13] William Bain asks:

> But if it is clear that English School theorists take history seriously, their purpose for doing so is a great deal less so. Once we have gotten inside history and have allowed our imagination to roam freely, we are still left to ask: What is historical knowledge for.[14]

It would be a drastic understatement to say creating an ES research programme would be challenging but it is necessary. The largest obstacle for the formulation of such a programme would be the three levels of analysis that are simultaneously involved in the School's tenets – system, international society and world society. Each level has its own concerns and understandings, though there is one key commonality in each – the role of the state – and this could easily serve as a starting point in building hard-core assumptions.

Identifying the hard-core assumption of a given research programme becomes essential in attempting to apply methodological and metatheoretical coherence to a theory. According to Lakatosian theory:

> All scientific research programmes may be characterized by their *hard core*. The negative heuristic of the programme forbids us to direct the *modus tollens* at this hard core. Instead, we must use our ingenuity to articulate or even invent auxiliary hypotheses, which form a *protective belt* around this core, and we must redirect the *modus tollens* to *these*. It is this protective belt of auxiliary hypotheses which has to bear the brunt of tests and get adjusted and re-adjusted, or even completely replaced, to defend the thus-hardened core. A research programme is successful if all this leads to a progressive problemshift; unsuccessful if it leads to a degenerating problemshift.[15]

The challenge posed by the English School would be trying to gain acceptance from School adherents that the state, and a monolithic view of the state at that, would be ideal as a hard core, and further, exactly where to apply certain assumptions given the multi-level analysis within the School. In an effort to demonstrate what such a programme would look like, it would be necessary to examine the international system, international society and world society.

The International System

- *Hard Core* – states are the primary actors in international politics.

The state in this level of analysis is closely related to the realist understanding, where states are understood as monolithic actors seeking to maximise their security and/or power and pursue their self-interest based on rational calculations of other actors' preferences. Hard-power capabilities are what differentiate states, not any conception of form.

- *Protective Belt of Auxiliary Hypotheses* – security and/or power maximisation is the underlying goal for states. As Waltz claims: 'In anarchy, security is the highest end. Only if survival is assured can states safely seek such other goals as tranquillity, profit, and power.'[16]

Assessing problem shifts in the systemic level would remain intra-programme shifts if they contributed novel facts about the centrality of the security-maximising state and did not betray the negative heuristic. Richard Ashley, for instance, focuses criticism at the systemic research programme proposed here by attacking the hard core:

> Excluded, for instance, is the historically testable hypothesis that the state-as-actor construct might be not a first-order given of international political life but part of a historical justificatory framework by which dominant coalitions legitimise and secure consent for their precarious conditions of rule.[17]

Such a claim would become degenerative to the research programme because of its attack on the programme's core assumptions. Instead, scholarship on balancing behaviour, forecasting ability, rationality of states and hard power considerations would likely adhere to the hard-core assumptions of the research programme. Inter-programme shifts would be disloyal to the negative heuristic and would attempt to alter hard-core assumptions. For instance, if states were removed as primary actors in international politics, if the existence and anarchic nature of the international system were brought into question, no novel facts would be contributed to such a research programme.

International Society

- *Hard Core* – states are the primary actors in international politics. States here, however, are not monolithic actors that are only concerned with hard power capabilities as defined in realist literature. Rather, the English School has varying notions of states and statehood, but international society adherents remain committed to the state as the primary actor through which international relations is conducted.

- *Protective Belt of Auxiliary Hypotheses* – security and/or power maximisation remains the primary goal of states, but security is maintained by dialogue, cooperation and institutional binding. The first concern for states is to survive in the international system, which means the establishment of some kind of hard power balance. Once this is achieved, states are able to use international society as a means to safeguard that hard power equilibrium and to capitalise on the other capabilities they may have.

Problem shifts in the theory of international society would be numerous and also difficult to assess. As long as the state remains at the centre of a theory, whether identified as pluralist or solidarist, it is likely to remain an intra-programme shift. This being said, any theory involving an international society should reject any overly world society-based arguments that seek to emphasise humanity over a system and society where states are the primary units of analysis.[18] The openness that the English School is so proud of is not totally closed by using Lakatosian logic; it just becomes easier for scholars to evaluate whether a contribution is providing novel facts or is actually degenerative. Tim Dunne asserts: 'It is clear ... that the term international society has been used by a variety of theoretical orientations as a general signifier of the institutional context within which interstate interactions take place.'[19] Dunne is correct to point out that English School foundations have been incorporated into the works of various theorists, but it is also important for those loyal to the English School to be able to identify when a theory is betraying its foundational elements.

By opening the concept of the state, this research programme is able to appreciate states' involvement in the international political economy, their sometimes irrational behaviour and institutional reliance and the conditions under which institutions must discuss the possibility of humanitarian intervention. In this sense, international politics remains a uniquely statist concern and states are perceived to act only when it is in their self-interest; at the same time, security and power are no longer strictly seen as hard power in nature given the heavily social elements of international society that in many ways equal or supersede traditional realist arguments in English School literature in determining or explaining state actions and outcomes. Each theory in this research programme should adhere to the basic identifying aspects of English School theory – the existence and importance of institutions, both primary and secondary. By doing so, one can more aptly identify a novel contribution to English School thought or dismiss it as degenerative.

World Society

- *Hard Core* – humans are the primary actors in global politics, but cannot achieve their ends without the existence of a strong and functioning international society.

States remain central to understanding the international arena, but world society is more concerned with the relationship between humans and the society of states. Securing individual rights and life become the primary tasks of states in all of their forms.

- *Protective Belt of Auxiliary Hypotheses* – human security is the end at which global politics aims, but states must be involved in finding ways to achieve this end. Without states and their involvement in institutions at the international society level, the impact of individuals is likely to be negligible.

The most contentious aspect of evaluating English School thought arises when world society becomes heavily involved.[20] In terms of security, contemporary discourse has become increasingly interested in the relationship of human security to the society of states. Progression in theoretical terms may bring the institutions of international society into question, but should not dismiss the predominance of the state or its role in protecting, or harming, the interdependent conception of humanity. In their description of Nicholas Wheeler's work, Bellamy and McDonald typify how solidarist studies provide novel facts to the English School research programme:

> However, although he argues that it is possible to conceive of situations where the security of individuals or communities should – and indeed does – take precedence over the security of states, he is reticent about how far these developments can go. He is therefore committed to retaining the state as the principle *agent* of security though he argues that individuals,

particularly individuals subjected to systematic abuse, should be the primary *referent*.[21]

The intention of this proposed English School Scientific Research Programme is to help scholars recognise when a theoretical contribution is either novel or degenerative. Theoretical plurality may be a positive aspect of using the English School approach in the first place, but in some cases it has become far too open and prevents the approach from entering the mainstream of international theory.

ES literature has, since the 1970s and 80s, had a strong preoccupation with world society and how international society interacts with humanity. This has led to many arguments about humanitarian intervention, civilisation, legitimacy, justice, and responsibility. Buzan claims that the reason for the world society emphasis was a shift from international to world.[22] Other School contributors have accepted this contention as almost a given reality, yet no attention has been given to empirically testing such a significant claim. Have states become less relevant and humanity more the focus of state behaviour? Have normative ideals of morality and cosmopolitanism become the driving forces behind the actions of international society?

This is not to say that the world society fixation is flawed, but rather speaks to the need for a methodological framework that allows observers to test the School's tenets and whether modern ES literature is adhering to the same hard-core assumptions as the School's organisers. Without being able to ask such questions, it may be that there is an English School discourse that includes references to international society, institutions and law without there actually being a coherent and organised school of thought.

Conclusion

All legitimate theories must stand up to testing in order for them to be taken seriously. To date, the English School has been limited in its appeal precisely because its adherents have little or no interest in operating according to a set of defined methodological rules. Without the value provided by methodological rigour, the School faces questions about its ability to be taken seriously as a *theory*. History might demonstrate that various international societies have existed, but where did they come from, how are they created and who determines whether a particular society of states can be identified either as solidarist or pluralist in nature? When do international societies change or collapse? Even within the ES itself, the solidarist vs pluralist division makes it difficult to answer why the School exists at all; it seems as if both sides of the debate assume that it is still relevant and adds something to the way international politics is explained, though *how* this is done is ambiguous.

Without any sort of method to evaluate its contributions to the field, what function does the ES serve in the broader scope of international theory? That is where Lakatos may be of assistance, in that his work helps scholars to explore 'how to assess theories, and how to decide whether, over time, theories about international relations are getting any better'.[23] Promoting a middle way of theory-making is not exclusive to the ES, as constructivism has more recently argued how to incorporate aspects of realism and liberalism into one approach, but constructivist scholars have dedicated themselves to answering questions about a constructivist methodology.[24] Within those identified as ES scholars, one can classify realists, liberals, Marxists, postmodernists, Frankfurt School proponents, constructivists and a variety of others, but other than a specific set of discursive elements and conceptual categories (international society, world society, etc.), how is one to prove these thinkers are contributing to the ES or conclude that a totally new series of research programmes has appeared since the end of the Cold War?

Until the practitioners of the English School begin to define precisely what an ES research programme would look like, the School's impact on international theory remains outside the mainstream. This is certainly not an effort to *Americanize* the English School but rather to hold the School to the same standards as other approaches to international relations. Martha Finnemore provides a succinct argument for why methodological concerns matter: 'Americans are fond of asking what the value added is of a theoretical approach: providing a strong demonstration of this for the English School would be powerful for that audience.'[25] Lakatos' work on research programmes would be immensely helpful in this regard because of its ability to allow for flexibility while still identifying either a single or a series of hard-core assumptions by which the School and its adherents would have to employ in order to demonstrate the School's theoretical impact on actual world events.

Notes

1. Dale Copeland, 'A Realist Critique of the English School', *Review of International Studies* 29 (2003), 431.
2. The main commonality between English School theorists is their use of the idea of international society. See Brunello Vigezzi, *The British Committee and the Theory of International Politics 1954–1985* (Milan: Edizione Unicopli Srl, 2005).
3. Richard Little, 'History, Theory and Methodological Pluralism in the English School', *Theorising International Society: English School Methods* (Houndmills: Palgrave, 2009), 78.

4. Roger Epp, 'The English School on the Frontiers of International Society', *The Eighty Years' Crisis: International Relations 1919–1999* (Cambridge: Cambridge University Press, 1998), 61.

5. For more on the School's reorganisation, see Barry Buzan, 'The English School: An Underexploited Resource in IR', *Review of International Studies* 27 (2001), 471-88.

6. Colin Elman and Miriam Fendius Elman, 'Lessons from Lakatos', *Progress in International Relations Theory* (Cambridge: MIT Press, 2003), 21-5.

7. Imre Lakatos, *The Methodology of Scientific Research Programmes* (Cambridge: Cambridge University Press, 1978), 94.

8. Ibid., 92.

9. Brendan Larvor, *Lakatos: An Introduction* (New York: Routledge, 1998), 45.

10. Lakatos, *Methodology of Scientific Research Programmes*, 35.

11. Mayall argues that the English School follows in the empiricist tradition of Locke and Hume, but notes this differs from the positivist method of empirically testing theory. See James Mayall, 'The Limits of Progress: Normative Reasoning in the English School', *Theorising International Society: English School Methods* (Houndmills: Palgrave, 2009), 211-12.

12. Copeland, 'A Realist Critique of the English School', 432.

13. For an interesting analysis of history in the English School, see William Bain, 'Are There Any Lessons of History?' *Review of International Politics* 44 (2007), 513-30.

14. William Bain, 'The English School and the Activity of Being an Historian', *Theorising International Society: English School Methods* (Houndmills: Palgrave, 2009), 148.

15. Lakatos, *Methodology of Scientific Research Programmes*, 48.

16. Kenneth Waltz, *Theory of International Politics* (New York: McGraw Hill, 1979), 126.

17. Richard Ashley, 'The poverty of neorealism', *Neorealism and its Critics* (New York: Columbia University Press, 1986), 270.

18. For more on the essential position of the state in international society, see Hedley Bull, 'The State's Positive Role in World Affairs', *Hedley Bull on International Society* (Houndmills: Macmillan, 2000), 139-56.

19. Tim Dunne, 'The New Agenda', *International Society and its Critics* (Oxford: Oxford University Press, 2005), 66.

20. This is primarily due to the inconsistency with which the term world society is used. See Richard Little, 'International System, International Society and World Society: A Re-evaluation of the English School', *International Society and the Development of International Relations Theory* (London: Continuum, 2002), 59-79.

21. Alex Bellamy and Matt McDonald, 'Securing International Society: Towards an English School Discourse of Security', *Australian Journal of Political Science* 39:2 (July 2004), 316.

22. See Barry Buzan, *From International to World Society? English School Theory and the Social Structure of Globalization* (Cambridge: Cambridge University Press, 2004).

23. Colin Elman and Miriam Fendius Elman, 'Lessons from Lakatos', 21.

24. An essential contribution to constructivist methods and theory making is found in Alexander Wendt, *Social Theory of International Politics* (Cambridge: Cambridge University Press, 1999).

25. Martha Finnemore, 'Exporting the English School?' *Review of International Studies* 27 (2001), 513.

Contributors

Alexander Astrov is Associate Professor at Central European University, Budapest. He is the author of *On World Politics: R.G. Collingwood, Michael Oakeshott and Neotraditionalism in International Relations* (Palgrave, 2005) and the editor of *Great Power (mis)Management: The Russian-Georgian war and its Implications for Global Political Order* (Ashgate, 2011).

Filippo Costa Buranelli holds a PhD in International Relations in the Department of War Studies, King's College London, where he is currently a Research Assistant and Teaching Fellow. He was awarded the English School Award for the Outstanding Paper presented by a Junior Scholar at the 2015 ISA Annual General Meeting. His research has been published in *Millennium*, the *Journal of Eurasian Studies* and *Global Discourse.*

Tim Dunne is Executive Dean of the Faculty of Humanities and Social Sciences and Professor of International Relations in the School of Political Science and International Studies at the University of Queensland. He is also a Senior Researcher in the Asia Pacific Centre for the Responsibility to Protect, a joint initiative between the University of Queensland and the Australian Department of Foreign Affairs and Trade.

Roger Epp is Professor of Political Science at the University of Alberta. His work includes *We Are All Treaty People* (2008), which reflects a larger interest in place and situated knowledge. His work on Martin Wight, the British Committee, applied hermeneutics, and the idea of the limit in international theory has appeared in numerous journal articles and edited collections, most recently *The English School Guide to International Studies* (2014).

Adrian Gallagher is an Associate Professor in International Security in the Department of Politics and International Studies at the University of Leeds. He uses an English School approach to study mass violence and has published articles in *Review of International Studies*, *International Relations*, *Global Responsibility to Protect* and *International Journal of Human Rights* amongst others. He also published *Genocide and Its Threat to Contemporary International Order* (Palgrave Macmillan, 2013).

Ian Hall is Professor of International Relations at Griffith University, Brisbane, Australia. He is the author of *The International Thought of Martin Wight* (Palgrave, 2006) and *Dilemmas of Decline: British Intellectuals and World Politics, 1945–1975* (University of California Press, 2012).

Tom Keating is a Professor Emeritus and former Chair of the Department of Political Science at the University of Alberta, where he has also served as Vice-Dean in the Faculty of Arts. He is the author of *Canada and World Order* (Oxford University Press, 2013) and also of *Global Politics, Emerging Networks, Trends, and Challenges* co-authored with Andy Knight (Oxford University Press, 2010).

Andrew Linklater is the Woodrow Wilson Professor of International Politics at Aberystwyth University in the UK. His most recent book is *The Problem of Harm in World Politics: Theoretical Investigations* (Cambridge University Press, 2011). The sequel, *Violence and Civilization in the Western States-Systems* will be published by Cambridge University Press in 2016.

Richard Little is a former editor of the *Review of International Studies* and a former chair of the British International Studies Association. He is now an Emeritus Professor at the University of Bristol and a Fellow of the British Academy.

Cornelia Navari is Emeritus Senior Lecturer at the University of Birmingham, UK and Visiting Professor at the University of Buckingham, editor of *Theorising International Society: English School Methods* (2009) and author of *Internationalism and the State in the 20th Century* (2000) and *Public Intellectuals and Foreign Policy* (2012).

Jason Ralph is Professor of International Relations at the University of Leeds, Honorary Professor at the University of Queensland and Marie Curie International Outgoing Fellow at the Asia-Pacific Centre for the Responsibility to Protect.

Yannis A. Stivachtis is Associate Professor of Political Science at Virginia Tech. He also serves as Head of the English School section of the International Studies Association (ISA). His most recent publications include: *Interrogating Regional International Societies, Questioning Global International Society* (editor, special issue of *Global Discourse*, 2015); *Europe after Enlargement* (co-editor, 2014); *Europe and the World: The English School Meets Post-colonialism* (editor, special issue of the *Review of European Studies*, 2012); and *International Order in a Globalizing World* (editor, 2007).

Cathinka Vik is an Assistant Professor in the Department of Health, Technology and Society at Gjøvik University College, Norway. Her primary research interests include collective security and global health in an international relations and international political economy perspective.

Matthew S. Weinert is Associate Professor in the Department of Political Science and International Relations at the University of Delaware. He is the author of *Democratic Sovereignty* (University College London, 2007), and *Making Human: World Order and the Global Governance of Human Dignity* (University of Michigan, 2015). His research focuses on the development of architectures of (global) governance that emerge at the intersection of state interests and human well-being.

John Williams is Professor of International Relations in the School of Government and International Affairs at Durham University, UK. His research work on the English School has concentrated on normative theory, particularly in relation to pluralism and the ways in which ethical diversity in world politics can be understood. This work has culminated in *Ethics, Diversity and World Politics: Saving Pluralism From Itself?* (2015 Oxford University Press) which seeks to fundamentally reform the pluralist strand of English School theory as a normatively progressive basis for understanding world politics beyond the society of states.

Note on Indexing

E-IR's publications do not feature indexes due to the prohibitive costs of assembling them. However, if you are reading this book in paperback and want to find a particular word or phrase you can do so by downloading a free e-book version of this publication in PDF from the E-IR website.

When downloaded, open the PDF on your computer in any standard PDF reader such as Adobe Acrobat Reader (pc) or Preview (mac) and enter your search terms in the search box. You can then navigate through the search results and find what you are looking for. In practice, this method can prove much more targeted and effective than consulting an index.

If you are using apps such as iBooks or Kindle to read our e-books, you should also find word search functionality in those.

You can find all of our e-books at: http://www.e-ir.info/publications

www.ingramcontent.com/pod-product-compliance
Lightning Source LLC
Chambersburg PA
CBHW072143020426
42334CB00018B/1863